DAVID HARSENT

Skin

faber

First published in 2024
by Faber & Faber Ltd
The Bindery, 51 Hatton Garden
London   EC1N 8HN

Typeset by Hamish Ironside
Printed in the UK by TJ Books Limited, Padstow, Cornwall

A CIP record for this book is available from the British Library

ISBN 978–0–571–38256–9

MIX
Paper from
responsible sources
FSC® C013056

Printed and bound in the UK on FSC® certified paper in line with our continuing
commitment to ethical business practices, sustainability and the environment.
For further information see faber.co.uk/environmental-policy

Contents

Fool, the king of spite. His laughter will find your wound.

STONES

[I]

Do you see how simple it is
Do you see how it sleeps in my hand
Do you see how it is part of sleep, its closed eye, its perfect silence, perfect because it evolved as silence and still holds, do you see how the depth of silence and the depth of sleep are one thing, and if the stone –

If the stone were broken open
There would be at the core limitless emptiness
The one idea certain to cure the world now gone to waste, a language lost that would have returned us to ourselves, the one image of God that the stone kept brought to light and the damage done, the sleeping God –

The sleeping God now woken
And calling to silence: wind over stone, fever-wind
And you are slow to breathe as rain hits the clitterfield blood-dark, as the run-off makes low-ground, goes to the hairline fractures, a rubble of feather and fur, of beak and bone, finds out the shallow graves –

[II]

The scaffold's counterweight
Is a granite block cut to the ounce and harnessed
In darkness ready to stall at the point of breakage, jittering, shocked by the
drop, caught in a timeless silence only stone can hold, stripped of moss,
lichen, snail-track, birdlime, unlike itself, transported, put to work –

Put to work as a navvy digs a ditch
Who thinks of the end of things as he feels the chill
To his back, as the blade breaks stone, this man knee-deep, he sings the
Hosannah Hymn, its beat a brace to his shoulders, thinks of the end of things
as a wild shout into light that might be soon, might come to him –

Might come to him in a dream
Of stone walls, a halter, the hymn, again
The hymn, a deadness which is lack of birdsong, lack of weather, his wife
beside him to reckon with his cries-in-sleep unless he beds down in the ditch,
stone his pillow, roots fresh-dug, that milky churchyard smell –

[III]

You find yourself eye to eye
With an angel dressed in white stone,
She has about her a sulky look and her hair is touchable; she seems pre-
occupied but you know she can hear you, can hear that you love her for her
blind eyes, her mouth because it offers up to kissing, nor does she flinch –

Nor does she when you trace the line
Of her cheek, her throat, let your hand then fall
To her breast, which tests cold and smooth and hard. Find her in church or
among broken pillars on a day of shadow-flood and sunlight: in that broken
glare she seems to spread her wings, but she's bedded in –

Bedded in with the dead
Or with you by the sea's edge skimming stones
Beside you waiting for a night train, at the market, a fruit-eater eyeing up the
prime cuts, at your door to play the uninvited guest, full length on your bed,
wings folded to a line of light, her hand between her legs –

[IV]

To Scorhill, to thoughts of the end of things,
A chill to your back as you lean against the kingstone
And look out to where faithless wives would come to wash in the ice-water of
the pool, circle the stones three times, then put themselves through the quoit
of Mên-an-Tol to purify, to pray for deliverance, to live or die –

To live and walk back across the moor
Sinless and scoured, the press of her breasts
Clear on the wet of her shift, her husband at the door to watch her come, new
to him now, while her lover holds that same image in the deep of his eye as she
will call to him under her breath, as her husband sets out –

To Scorhill, carrying mallet and wedge
To split a stone for the deadweight, no thought
Of the voice in stone or the man who will take the drop giving Hosannah
Hosannah under his breath. In the house daylight is half-light. She stands
between bed and kitchen, glad to be nameless in that nameless place –

[V]

Stone hides itself in itself and thinks itself
Invisible. Its breathing is the near-death rhythm
Of hibernation. There is nothing of this in the word stone; and everything.
The word of God is stone. Your lover's last look back is stone. You take stone
to your heart. You lift a stone from the beach and it fits your hand –

Fits just so, is sure to find its match
In the way your fingers close and make a seal,
The rub of salt to flesh (augur of sin, so quick in memory), how it leaches heat
from your skin, reads your palm, tests your smell, measures your heartbeat,
settles to sleep, as stones roll in the wavebreak, as daylight dies –

Dies touch by touch and you are left to chance,
To moonrise, to what you know of bones and the sea,
Of the bloodless shapes that come to you in dream. The stone is at your bed-
side between the book you have set aside and the photograph of your children
who can never, now, be called back from the world –

[VI]

A place where visions come
In stillness out of wavebreak, the skyline
A running flame, a firestorm on the surface of the sea and a sudden billow
moves with the swell towards the shore where the air is ash and coals,
unbreathable, as bedrock heaves and splits, as the sky burns –

The sky burns. There are men walking
At the sea's edge, men of coals and ash, their footfalls
Scorch the stones, a wind off the sea stirs them to flame, they let go a litter of
fire, airborne, that becomes a circle of birds, wings outspread, burnt black, and
from somewhere a chorus of voices telling all this –

All this held in a fierce harmony
You said, the vision come and gone in an eyeblink
As you stood at the tideline, stunned, locked off from all other sights and
sounds. Later you lay in bed, set in the deep of your eye the image that soon
went to dream: sea, sky, birds, boots on broken stone –

[VII]

She opens the door a fraction, then
A fraction more: opens it on a whisper
Since she has it in mind to slip in beside you and please you as you sleep,
slowly, wordlessly, keeping her face turned from you, although you'd know her
by her touch and the deep sweet smell she brings to the task –

The task you will hold in memory
On waking, the touch but more the smell. Of course
She has seen the hagstone, her token, strung up on the lintel; she reached to it
as she came in and the room sank back to darkness. She is your lover's lover;
she reads your names as palindromes, yourselves a mirror image –

Mirror image face to face, a smudge
Of shadow between: her mark, spit or sweat
Or press of lips . . . Her fingers rest on your eyelids, a means of capture, her
breath narcotic as she leans in. If you could see how your skin puckers at her
touch, could hear your shout as she spreads and straddles you –

[VIII]

A witch's thumbstone has been left
On the windowsill as if to catch the light; a pattern
Of scarring – see there? – on the underside where it turned in a mash of
foam and broke open, the upperside rubbed smooth year after year when she
brought on her other self, near sleeping it seemed –

Near sleeping as she sang
Under her breath to bring to its best
The linctus for grippe, for flux, foul-sweat, quinsy, brakebone, sang to women
in labour, to men under the knife, sang at the fever-bed, sang as best she was
able given the plum-dark blemish and twist to her jaw –

The twist and broken teeth
Where the scold's bridle choked back
Her scream as they brought the branding iron to her arm. Later she kept the
stone under her thumb as she sang their names, spat after each, turned in a
circle, soft-footed, her little solo firelit dance of death –

[IX]

A presentiment of death that settled in you
Like a stone, stone-cold and deep. Midwinter, pale light,
Foxtracks on the riverside path. 'Why do we write at the tip of the world's end,
tell me, why do we write if everything will burn? I have dreams, but some-
times visions. I want to shake them off but they go with me to give sight –

Give sight of a day when birds will roost
In daylight, the wind drop to silence, and silent
Shapes, that want to be anything or anyone, drift in a found darkness: they
shift and smudge, yes, and give sight of a white bed in a white room, the sound
of small machines, time holding back as if it might soon fail –

Will soon fail and the room then fold
Like paper to make an origami hare, and that is my dream
Of death. I sometimes think the fire on the seam of the sea that falls into sight
as I come close to sleep must be hell-fire, and firewalkers the true prophets.
There has been a fox here. Look. This is a blind light –'

[X]

There's an echo trapped under this capstone
A shout overlaid by a howl, fluctuating music of the hunt,
Which you might get as tremor if you flatten your hand on the surface, tremor
or something more like an itch. If there had been bones among the ash, if
there had been a torc, a ring, a dogtooth amulet (as you imagine it) –

You imagine it as on the day they lit
The pyre and hollowed out the cyst and set the stones,
The day turf was cut for the mound and his name was lost. As you sit close
by, eyes closed, holding that image, something flies in, touches down, lifts off:
something big is all you can tell since your eyes stay shut –

Eyes shut, one hand on the stone, the other
Over your mouth in case the echo should rise
In you and break through and everything change. What might come of this
now you have it in memory, now you know the place, now nothing will shift
the itch? It must have been a hawk, a crow, an owl unlucky in daylight –

[XI]

Think, now, of the music in stone; think
Of what song a stone might sing. The moor at first light
Is a running sea and you in the midst as if going naked into the tideline chop,
the sea bed shelving under your feet, a chill to your skin that sends you further
out, your mind coming clear, the sky unfolding where you look up –

Look up at a circling sunstruck bird
Fire from its pinions kindling the moorland gorse;
A web holds water-beads: broken wheel of reflections as you go through with-
out purpose or plan except that you want the deep of the moor as you want the
deep of the tide, the songline between land and sea –

Between land and sea and sky
Province of the goddess, where you're held
In a moment of blindness and there comes on the air, somehow drawn down,
a monotone of catastrophic beauty that could upturn the world, could bring
the world to its knees in sin, and that is the music in stone –

[XII]

The heaviness in this is corpse-love.
This is burdened by the incalculable weight
Of an empty womb. This carries hatred and will never be rid of it. In this one,
pain and in this and this and this, pain turned in on itself, pain at the heart of
things, pain's glee, pain's box of tricks, pain God's gift to the world –

God's gift a great cairn raised
In a hidden place in a nameless wilderness
Each stone weighed down by its payload, human, inhuman, denatured, some-
thing gone that was no more than itself buried in itself, was its own dead
centre, was darkness veiled by darkness and a profound silence –

Silence so profound that it lay
Beyond measure. Now the stones believe
A language has been lost to them of guilt and redemption; they want to strike
out at themselves, they are dream-afflicted, they imagine patterns in the wind
that they take to be God's curse, they are given to all this for all time –

[XIII]

There's a worm that eats stone and shits sand.
It is pale and blind, something like a leech or a slug,
Viscous, gut-visible, it would fit the length of your hand from heel to fingertip
if you could bring yourself to pick it up, but don't keep that image too long in
mind (pale and blind and hollow-mouthed) or it will go deep –

Go deep and give voice, much like
Whalesong, but distant, thin, what a stone would hear
If stones could fear death, if they had stoneworm dreams, if they caught a
sudden pulse, voice-become-shockwave, and tried to call a warning because
the beat of that airborne word was *rockdrill-rockdrill-rockdrill* –

Rockdrill-rubble, wormcasts, silt
Of shed skins, litter of wings and beaks
In a fractured landscape picked over by vermin, the sea drawn back beyond
the skyline and gone to shallows, the sun an agony, the moon shuttered, and
this apocalypse the last and worst of the stoneworm myth –

We are impelled to pick up

a pebble shaped by the sea

because it is just-so

Marie-Louise von Franz

SALT MOON

[I]

This last view of the sea. This vastness. Flood of light.
As you might be a bird, mid-air and flying blind,
eyes whitened by airborne salt

riding a storm wind, numb with loss, empty
of purpose, stolen from yourself,
the high vision occluded, nothing but this blank

reach of moonlight sealed on the skim, and what
was hidden from you then is hidden still
blind to moonlight, blind to landfall, blind to the rising sun

nothing but dream and drift, a bird's idea of flight
all that's left of instinct, cold thin blood,
updraught to wingspan: so caught, you soar into darkness.

[II]

Maris stella . . . profer lumen cæcis

In reach of land, a bird stalls to make a blind
turn to the open sea; can you find it: white
on white-on-black, near-lost in the moon's reflection

as you walk the foreshore, drawn to the breakers, and
under the tireless gaze of this black Madonna, Star
of the Sea, her shrine a break in the cliff face where

the last of the lost give themselves over to sorrow.
Knee-deep, you feel the frenzy of shoreline stones
in the draw of the tide; take one: its heart

is that frantic pulse on your palm; strike out:
you and you alone are here for this.
Deepwater silence, white-eyed fish, a huddle of dimlit bones.

[III]

Here is a table covered in black oilcloth. On the table
a white bowl shaped and marked like the moon. You stand
a little way off, your back to the window: twelve small panes

that frame twelve views of a salt moon. The oilcloth
carries a wash of white light, as a shrine might carry
a single light, untouched, untouchable. The bowl

sits dead centre, somehow holding together
a perfect fragility, and now to say *bowl*, soft spherical O,
is to cup it in your hands, slant to the sea-wind

stones shifting under your feet, stones in the draw
of the tide, you alone, and the bowl stirring
as a sleeping thing might stir, taking the light, an opening eye.

[IV]

The bird is moonblind; those subtleties are lost to it. Cold blood.
Heart of stone. Adrift in darkness. You alone know this.
If only it could fold its wings. If only it could make

landfall to roost in its own stain. If it could sleep.
Imagine a dream of falling, fathomless. You grow
old in the dream. In the dream you outlive yourself.

A room in a house on a cliff where you find your face
in each of twelve small windowpanes
and the moonbowl, white on black, and a silent sea.

The wave-top cataract is a measure of heartbreak.
The house is stitched with secrets, as you know.
The bird is held on the wind, voiceless crucifix.

[V]

The black Madonna

The music she hears night-long, as you alone
know, is wind across broken stone where
she waits on the sea's leavings –

plastic and rope and tin and glass and white-eyed fish
gill-choked in the ghost net, and bones
fetched up from the deep by the deep draw of the tide –

which she takes to be votives: her hand upraised to bless.
All she knows is sea and what sea brings, salt moon
her benediction. There is nothing to be got from her

save that her mantle folds and falls across
wishbone shoulders, that her eyes can drink the light,
that one by one her sorrows dance in silence.

[VI]

Moonrise: cloud grows thin and tears. A slop of white
light falls to the swell. The bird flies low to the chop
and takes the shine to its breast, as your face silvers,

as the windowpanes gloss, as the patterns shift
and settle, as the house now shifts and settles.
The seaward room is the only room; the only door

opens onto wave-break and the cliff edge; so lean
into the onshore wind, it will nail you there,
arms spread, a shadow-shape, your song

flung back at you . . . *ave* . . . *ave* . . . and soon the drop
opens beneath your feet to give
rockfall, a running sea, the moon haloed in mist.

[VII]

The sea's death-haul decays under this spillage of light.
Picked clean and turned aside. Picked clean and left to lie.
Picked clean and nameless now, sea-junk like the rest

plastic and rope and tin. A night-flying bird
leaves its shadow on shoreline stone as it lifts
into the wind. Moonlight hardens; its pitch-and-pull

on the wavetop, unreadable, is the hidden hand of God
as you alone know, has always been, will always be,
so wind and water have cut that break in the cliff face

from where she marks each phase of the moon, each turn
of the tide, night-long vigil, stopless silence, unshakeable
stillness of contemplation, she will never tire of you.

[VIII]

One wall in the house is papered with views of the sea,
the opposing wall with times of tides and moonrise,
the far wall facing the windowpanes is a ravel of water-lights.

There is music from somewhere, backwash music,
untraceable, your hands in front of your face,
the drop, the draw of the sea, the skyline rinsed

by the last light of the day, how the turn of the tide
seems to fold the moon's reflection, how
that crease in dark water deceives, how trash

on the shoreline is sited and set with a flourish as
the waves pull back, how those patterns break and remake,
how your song is at odds with the music.

[IX]

Watch how the water rises to the light
to draw it down, to draw it on, to let it slip
into the trough, to have it ride the shoulder of the wave . . .

What do you bring to this? Even now, you might
wade in until your legs go out from under you,
might swim slow strokes through the slick,

might float face up, your eyes
soon to be white from looking too much at the moon;
and even now you might glean from the tideline dross

a handspan of glass rolled by the sea and scored
with scratch-mark hieroglyphs:
lost lines written by the blind for the blind.

[X]

As you might be a bird fording thin air to find
the line where night meets day as day declines,
gliding along that crest to reach its pitch

then tipping into the thermal drift to sleep
on the wing, a night-long shallow stoop, soft-boned, so you
could crumple in a headwind, while your dream

is shapes and distances, is patterns of sky that flow
above patterns of sea, and you somehow
held between them, dark in darkness, save

for that glint striking your eye which must be moonlight
swamping a cloudstack, as you wake
to spindrift and rack your wings and turn into the wind.

[XI]

Broken stone, from where she counts the hours; broken stone
as *vesica piscis*, as sacred geometry, as earth-shadow cast
across the moon, as mantle, as shroud, as her womb in blossom,

a shoreline altar laid with driftwood crosses, tin fish, the holy
accidental, where midnight communicants kneel
on flint and porphyry and quartz, sweet pain echoing from each

to each and music, too, going between them unheard, scars
reopening under the weight of pity, pity's gift,
the sea at their backs, its promise of redemption,

how they might be first picked clean then left to lie,
sinless, scoured by grace, lost to themselves at last, herself
as mediatrix, cold blessing of the salt moon.

[XII]

The house of secrets under a full moon

The windowpanes take the reflection of a bird
flying blind from light into light; its wings clatter the glass.
The wash on the far wall forms, reforms, sometimes

mouths, sometimes eyes, sometimes angels,
sometimes devils. Secrets are given and sworn,
pacts made that can't be kept: to walk into the deep

going side by side, to abandon everything, to lock
the only door and sit in silence, heads bowed, and wait it out.
The house rings in the wind. That sound

is the only music; it will play night-long (as you know)
loop-tape to match the moon's lightspool
and the window-glass a notch from breaking-point.

[XIII]

The moon a hagstone now, its sea-light turning on a dead
centre, blind eye, as it sheds to the tide-race. You look
out from the wall of windows, stand tiptoe where the cliff

drops into darkness, go down to the shoreline miracle
of rockfall and sea, drawn by the bright
seams folding, refolding against the swell . . .

and something of sorrow, something of fear
in that lock-and-release, eternal, as of cloud, as of leaf,
the night-bird patterning the dark, backwash

music of wave-break, wind across broken stone
which is evidence of absence, evidence of loss, yourself
unfound in that vastness of sea and land and light.

Solve vincla reis
profer lumen caecis
mala nostra pelle
bona cuncta posce

Break our chains
bring light to the blind
what is evil in us
take to yourself

Ave maris stella
Marian hymn, ninth century

HAUNTINGS

music that echoes darkness   *(3rd visitation)*

Have you noticed what their mouths do when they sing?
Something furtive about those silent shapes, the way
their hands drift in and out of sight. They draw together
as if they meant to, as if they might bring to the deepest
reaches of the night music that echoes darkness, its burden
a near-memory of some long lost thing, for a moment
holding bright, then disappeared. Fear stacks up. Sleep
is a cordon. Knowing this is what sets you apart.

First light hangs in trees before it finds your window
dead white, bone white against the glass. Winter dawn.
Do you feel that shift in the weather? A headache.
Iron breaking your eyeline. What drifts in that only you
can gather; yes, and that delirium of song: if heard,
some measure of sorrow; if unheard, heartbreak.

it shakes the air   *(4th visitation)*

They make use of the way light falls on floors, on walls,
the way it breaks across a door half open – the way it bends
and breaks. On one side of the door that comes to mind
they wait their turn, singing a forgotten narrative,
soundless; it shakes the air; you'd learn, if it came clear,
how they've remade it line by line and changed
her name and his. Even so, it's nothing new or brave:
fear and rage and love and sin and shame, all as before.

They are backed up to the door and listening. You might
think them man and wife. No. They're as people
who meet in a city backstreet, lost, and turn up here
by force of will, expecting to be somewhere safe.
Just as in life. Just as you search in sleep for the place
where you paused and looked back and were overwhelmed.

a fine disguise   *(5th visitation)*

This is their dance aetherial: caught in a pale rhomboid of light,
themselves creatures of light so if you glance and glance away
there's only a blue-white graze behind your eyes, that and the line
they take (almost too faint to trace) step-and-step-and-break:
a rhythm returning dream-knowledge of when that still unnamed
half-made thing turned from you while you slept, the shock
of abandonment self-locked and sealed with your other name
who might now be blamed for the traffic of souls in the night.

They are hooded or else go naked: a fine disguise, and reach
a sudden stillness in the dance that brings in this tragic poise,
this agony of touch. Think back. A gallery somewhere in France
you held by a charcoal sketch so slight it seemed to lack
everything but hint. It made you feel unsafe, you said, and then,
later, in a roadside bar, 'Whatever it was will haunt me all my life.'

just so, and soundless   *(6th visitation)*

You dream of the room where you sleep when you sleep in the room.
In the dream, you're asleep and dreaming of the room
as it will be when you wake: just so, and soundless. Soon enough
it will shed your warmth. The mirror will pick you up and let you go.
There are patterns that now and then shift. There are words unspoken.
In the drift of days, trees come into leaf. Crow Moon, Hare Moon.
There are promises made to be broken. Mysteries of misrule.
Apnoea wakes you. A trick of the light from the transom brings them in.

See them fleshed: subtle pornography. See them whole: you can't.
See them exchange a look and part and disappoint. No.
No. There is only blue-white light – a song given in silence –
the small perfections of the dance – that they like to be watched –
that they can't be heard or touched – that they arrange themselves
for you as shapes in air – that all of it and none of it is strange.

sometimes a bruise   *(7th visitation)*

Rainfall, the window mists, clack and clatter of knucklebones
against a wall. Put on the light. Adjust your shadow. Track
fragments of memory: this: you turn a corner to find yourself
trapped in the gesture, as if you had something more to give;
this: a woman crosses a busy street, her eyes on you, the future
builds in broken moments at her back; this: being schooled
in death, how it will come on a day like any other; this:
the tabs lift on a sad two-hander for recidivist and scold.

Sometimes a smudge in air, sometimes a bruise, sometimes
the way air travels when a door is thrust open or slammed,
unfolding to make an edge or drape, much as smoke unravels
and though they are nothing like smoke there's a drip-feed
playback of yourself turning that corner, feeling the sudden
drop in temperature, heartbeat, vision, slow stall in the blood.

it runs under the skin *(8th visitation)*

Now they are winged, or seem so. It lasts a minute or two.
They come in at a glide. That ragged blue is almost shape
before it fades. In the guise of angels, so you hide your face.
The image holds in the way something looked at long will hold.
It comes at you cold and runs under the skin: you might be ill
or this is the first wild lick of madness; go back, go back to when
birds were only birds if you spoke their names out loud,
then animals, then trees, until you wept: *Just words . . . just words . . .*

Crow. Hare. Rowan. Kestrel. Blackthorn. Fox. You drank
all day and stayed awake: a markless blank between
day and night, sleepless dreams, remorse, fear of the dark . . .
A woman there was to keep you from yourself; she said
Close your books, turn that picture to the wall, a shadow
will lift from you. Now they separate, made false by fracture.

# of something unrevealed *(9th visitation)*

Bell book and candle back then: back then aspergillum,
signum crucis, the priest's black look, his talk of pestilence,
infestation, that you brought it on yourself
with lust and lies, that they come to wait for your soul
to be given up from the most foul of the seven portals while
you sleep, fooled by dreams of deliverance, and wake
bright-eyed, feverish, hollowed by ecstasy, which thought
brings him to your side shaking with rage and need.

Imagine a double portrait of vacancy face to face.
Imagine it white. Imagine a brushstroke that comes
a moment too late, profiles that break and float, that tend
always to absence. Imagine a sunlit mirror, the cut-and-fold
of a double-take, sly reflection of something unrevealed.
Imagine them set in a sealed room, lost to the inner-eye.

as light will smear a screen   *(10th visitation)*

The room is a box just as any room is a box. So it is
that you are boxed in with them. Their eyes leave tracks,
or seem to. Maybe this time they'll mark the wall as light
will smear a screen and spill. And this is new: something
hard-borne which could be anger, sorrow, distress, you feel
the press of it on the air, you drag the sheets over your head,
you fall into that familiar dream of popinjay and hag,
her weird, her scars and spells, the seven colours in his coat.

Wake up. Get up. Turn your back. Open the door
as if there were nothing stopping you. Take your book
into the garden. Read. Set it aside. Go out. Notice how
you walk to a pattern: magic steps. Give up. Go home.
Trace the hidden ritual as you move from room to room.
What shape does it make? What dance? Where are they now?

this brings them to song (11th visitation)

Set them in a concert hall to tread the silences. Set them
in your childhood bedroom but to no good end. Set them among
headless angels in the old cemetery: this brings them to song
or so you think. Set them on the M-way overpass in dying sunlight:
you drive half blind. Set them in the garden at dusk: unseen
but watching. You wait for whatever will come, whatever risk
they bring, knowing it's too late to guess or care. You set them
white on white. You join them there. You wait to feel unwell.

The blackthorn comes into flower. Blackthorn and dog-rose. Blackthorn
and dog rose and broom. Between toppled headstones
a rough sleeper's fire gone cold. A fox has left its pawprints in the ash.
Read the names on the stones, imagine what pleasure-pain
exchange they made with the few who claimed to love them.
Blackthorn. Ash-fox. White on white. Cold flame.

given over to silence *(12th visitation)*

Residue, perhaps; pain's overspill. They think you live in fear.
They think they are here to bear witness. They think you think
you are old beyond your years. Memory's run-off, perhaps; detritus.
Words given over to silence; images that won't (will never) hold.
That same tree is moving in the wind, that same small river
is shelving over stone, whether you have them in mind or not.
Solitude's wastage; dregs of the heart, perhaps. There are places
yet to be found (but not by you) where the lost can start again.

The loudest bird is the wren, the wren at daybreak, doubling
between the ivy and the firethorn with all her magic intact.
You on your knees somehow. The sheet a rope. A wild morning:
sun and rain as one: 'the Devil is beating his wife'; 'a green
winter makes for a fat churchyard'. Now they think
those rhythms have marked your days. Touchstone, perhaps.

in the company of children   *(13th visitation)*

It might be that slow erasure is their way, something like
diminution by decay, how memory fails, how pleasure
becomes a black spot in the back-brain. That they flow
or seem to; that they warp, or seem to; that they gain
themselves by soft disfigurement. A day of rain comes first
to mind, the rest falls into place, the full weight of it
leaving you hard pressed. *O* . . . Time's deceits
will break you in the end. They might have guessed.

Think back to ratholes in the floor, to days spent weeping
in the company of children who outwept you. Anger like a sore
that had the run of your body. Anger and fear. Anger and fear
and despair. They guessed: and shape the pain as grace,
sometimes as gift. Kept secrets, the dead days of your parole.
Whisky-blind. Rats in the wallspace. Rats over the bed at night.

you fold into corners as you turn   *(14th visitation)*

You pace the room at night. Your shadow shifts. The light
is constant. Yes . . . What seems commonplace is never that.
This small-hours psychodrama in black and white holds up
in dreams as in the fastness of your room. Notice how you fold
into corners as you turn, sharp-edged, and then make good;
how what you shed is more and less of you; how shapes reshape.
Solo shadowplay; insomniac gavotte. Now sit on the bed,
fold your hands, look nowhere. Yes . . . Eidolon as silhouette.

To die unshriven and alone is nothing new. Make them
psychopomps to find you and lift you and take you at the last.
Their song of missed beats comes almost breathless, your voice
as descant, that long held note which could be a call on God
if räle is prayer. Here where your sins collect. Hands steepled
and cold. Slow-drawn veil. Birdsong. Nothing new. Expect it.

glass held up to glass   *(15th visitation)*

False dawn. Rainfall is lace on webs that hang from the iron rail
outside your window. Sunlight spills through it: water and fire.
You are the coldest, palest version of yourself, the least loved.
They make the shape of a hawk hunting its acres; this lasts
for as long as it takes to think it might have happened. They make
the shape of a dove. Your mistake is to look for meaning in this
or furtive beauty in the way they drape (or seem to)
fire-and-water selves across the mirror, glass held up to glass.

You sit in the garden and imagine the room as your oubliette –
bare floor, shelf-bed, web of bars, a narrow skylight set
high in the corner – and decorate the walls with a gallows-tree,
a fool's marotte, a line of song, your other name, all etched
into the stone with a key that will lock but not unlock.
The skylight empty of sky. A line of song etched into the bone.

awkward in the mirror   *(16th visitation)*

Their palette is greys and whites. Grey of ageing, white
of effacement; trace elements of sorrow and a white book,
your best and last. You go to them with a formal blessing
and a morning whisky: exorcism or test, yourself now
as outcast, the room afloat and adrift, a failing voice
that might well be your own, a returning face wide-eyed
and awkward in the mirror. The glass has grown
a second skin; it shivers; they ride that fever, then fade.

In cold sunlight, in a cutting wind, and you carry an image
that is bare contour, too thin to hold a shape, wind-whipped.
Walk to the sea. Find a boat. Make landfall. Board a train
to a place you've never heard of. Take a room in any street.
Bed down. Wake to their silent singing and the dance.
So now it completes. You are lost in them as they are lost in you.

they play bare-faced jack   *(penultimate visitation)*

There is more to be said of the soul-death of the High,
more to be said of the way their ghost-selves gather
by seats of power, boardrooms, Pall Mall clubs,
whorehouse lobbies, casinos where they play
bare-faced jack or knucklebones and watch the clock,
always on call should they catch the aftershock when
their host feels a blood-seep grow behind the eyes,
or cancer cells break open like a flower to the sun.

You think of your soul as the heart of a wren. It sits below
your own heart. *O!* Its pulse is troubled music.
Ghost-selves. An account of sin. Backlog of debt and harm.
You think of what their mouths do when they sing,
of step-and-step-and-break, of nothing but hint.
'Whatever it was will haunt me all my life.'

Wahr spricht, wer Schatten spricht.

Paul Celan, *Sprich Auch Du*

ANIMALS SILENT IN DARKNESS

Where they stand

How strange a thing: to kiss. He puts his mouth on hers.
A bonded breath. Blind each to each.
It's slow and troubled. Then light rushes in.

*

The rook that attends the moment is 'black as night'.
The tree where it comes to roost is stone.
Stone is shed where they stand, one on one, to kiss.

*

Here is the photograph. She put her mouth on his.
Light has spoiled the edges: there's a bleed.
The tree is the only tree. The rook is the only bird.

The sea wall

His hand a little anchor on her breast.
She gets up and goes out. Winterlight.
Risk in everything they do.

*

Usual patterns of silence, perhaps,
or some small wound has opened.
She turns to him. He is singing under his breath.

*

A year ago: he's on the sea wall, smoking;
she's ankle-deep in the tidewash.
It seemed to blur, just as this blurs now.

Souvenirs

Live music at the terminus, whistles and drums.
They are back from a place they found by chance.
Notes tap the roofglass then fall to silence.

*

She is mindful of her womb: a sudden weight
and bunches her fist to take account of it.
Some things are agreed but never spoken of.

*

They won't go there again, not for the basement bars
not for tower blocks topping the sun.
They came away, at last, with these mirrors and beads.

The snare

There are unexpected noises, mostly at night.
She reads while he sleeps.
The room as a cube of light, herself boxed in.

*

She gets up on her knees to kiss him (deep
kiss and long; her tongue might be a snare).
He almost wakes. Her lightest touch is theft.

*

Now and then, she fabricates his dreams. 'Did I talk?'
he asks. 'Yes, you talked.' 'What did I say?' 'You said,
Return from sin in sorrow. You said, Dust in the sun.'

The railing

They find themselves up at the edge (clifftop, rooftop,
tower); they play the fool with leap-and-drop.
It wasn't planned. There are accidental pathways.

*

Here is the knee-high railing. Here is the five-mile view
that fades to clifftops and rooftops and towers.
She puts a hand to his back and her cervix swamps.

*

It's possible to lie and be misunderstood. It's possible
to write your life in a single line: she told him so. The dream
version of this is cloudrace, the setting sun sketched in.

Under one roof

She faces up to the mirror and speaks the spell three times.
Certain words transpose. That shift
is a rogue heartbeat; she is losing sight of herself.

*

Nine charnel grounds. The image folds, unfolds, refolds. She works
the pattern out from the centre inch
by inch: there's unheard music. The roofbeams throw a web.

*

Dromenon, rose window, mandala, soft undertone spoken
on an indrawn breath, breath on the mirror
between herself and herself, what she wanted, just that, nothing else.

Fragments

His touch seethes in her even now. She walks into the dead
centre of a field where there is only sky, where sky
bears down on her, the pale before daybreak.

*

If things go right, she'll be invisible
and stop at every window so to learn
how secrets might be shared and understood.

*

'Translate to song what I kept back
from those parts-of-days.' He says he will, and will. As if
mirrors could store scenes like shadowplay.

In progress

What he does he does under cover, under pressure, holding
the image of a tide coming fast across a mile
of packed sand: that sudden shock as sea and sky collide.

*

He is mantling his work as a hawk will mantle the stricken
songbird and strip the belly-feathers and strip the skin.
He seems to not move and yet the bare bones shine.

*

He will sleep if he can. First he will drink, then sleep.
Release, desertion, abandonment, something of that . . .
Second thoughts might wake him before dawn.

Footsteps

A storm is riding the shoulder of a hill. Frost breaks out on grassland.
They share this or they will. Animals silent in darkness.
Their footsteps in a place they were meant to come to.

*

They could lie down anywhere and be gathered to stillness.
Not in one another's arms, that's an illusion.
In truth, it's an axis of absence: sorrow for sorrow.

*

They walk in open country hoping for rainfall
to complete the picture. Look out from this upper window.
There they are hand in hand and plain to the naked eye.

Handout

All this denial, all this half-formed pain, this landmark,
this severance, this same look back as she swivels
on the ball of her foot: bridge or entrance hall or Underground.

*

For example, the Underground – his slow diminishment.
Dark corridors, the din of machines, the tannoy-echo.
In legend she follows and finds him and brings him back.

*

Her pivot-turn stays in the air: shape, yes, but spasm too.
Beggars on the bridge lean in as she passes.
Please. Please. Please. They are unforgiveable.

In snow

He circles her: full-face, profile, back. This she allows
but doesn't break pace. He is her satellite, her moon. Imagine
what tracks they leave in the snow, of love and contradiction.

*

Frost in the air catches the back of her throat. She weeps
frost-tears. Full-face, but he doesn't see that. They cross
a running stream. Not all signs are symbols.

*

She is out of kind, as if weather might somehow fail her.
This is his route. Hers is further from home.
In the fresh fall he crosses, recrosses, full-face / profile / back.

Palais

Dancing like this, they might wrong-foot each other. And have.
They dip and rise and turn and dip and rise. His smile
falls just short of her. The music is in their heads, slow and particular.

*

The waxed floor and the unlit chandelier. There are flowers
in cut-glass bowls. There are fault-lines
that widen as they dance. The flowers are closed, as if against the night.

*

Cut glass. She sings the only note that goes to weakness,
sweet spot of fracture, the way
a finger might touch a wound and worsen it.

Edge

Sixteen windows here that wait on nightfall
and the soft cascade of lamplight. No change in that.
What was broken then is broken now.

*

The city boils up round them. Rim-glow of neon,
of sodium, of tower blocks, street signs, billboards, trucks . . .
Window-bars throw shadows where they sit.

*

They keep each other close: the only way
to still their demons. First light, dead light, cold rain
on rooftops, smokestacks, that clockwork diorama.

Scar

His hand goes there and comes back fast.
She makes a solemn joke of it.
The stories they tell about themselves end well.

*

It's noiseless where they are. They people the streets
with chancers, jokers, lovers on the run
each with a holdall, each with a one-way ticket.

*

What will you do when there's no time left for us? She'd like
to make a joke of it but lacks the guile.
What will you do when I can't tell day from night?

Close

Just a handspan between them, a handspan, maybe less,
as animals scent illness or rage. The wet
on his lip is hers; that on hers is his. They are lost in the near.

*

Face to face in the mirror. Their sightlines cross.
A rash of light plays back from the glass
and strikes their eyes. Lost to each other, then.

*

Closer still, but that was years ago. Her look
is curative, or wants to be. Something shifts. He turns
a corner; she goes from room to room. They are lost.

Art

When she first looks it's a bowl of figs
on a red check tablecloth and a half-glass door half open
onto the garden. When she looks back it's heartbreak.

*

Footsteps on bare boards in a slow revolve. As if
they left tracks. As if, in a room of strangers,
they might lose sight of each other and that the end of it.

*

Where they stop is an iron bridge that takes to its underside
a river-water glow that dances in green.
Someone drowning would see it much the same.

Linnet

Just as it was: the arcade, untraceable music,
a wind gathering trash.
To one side, gems; to the other, *haute couture.*

*

And a dog tethered to a railing. And a man
in a monogrammed apron swabbing tiles.
I remember, she says; what happened after that?

*

And a caged bird. Their promises can't be kept.
In bed they go back to back and Janus-faced:
that tell-tale chink in his smile, the dark of her eye.

Rain

She lays out fish and fruit and sets a fire. A circle
of stones, quartz by candlelight.
All on a whim; hexensabbat, as if by chance.

*

They wake as one to the cry of someone falling
pitched hard and high; a long fade into silence.
The contagion of dream. Images cross and collide.

*

She puts on the light and pours drinks
from the bottle kept by the bed.
How rain beats on the window patterns what they say.

The choice

It's a story yet to be told. In one account, they come
to somewhere trackless. Echoes of their voices,
made years ago, overlap and contradict and spoil.

*

Their lies are like for like and given cold. What next?
That sky and sea are seamless in reflection.
That they need to choose which of themselves to love.

*

Doors open onto doors. Rooms remake as replicas.
Streets run in parallel. Nothing else. Or they
turn wise and unrepentant and go where they must.

Near night

Fingertip to fingertip, trembling, testing voltage.
They're in search of endurable pain. Eyes shut,
speechless, going by touch – by touch, as before.

*

The fall of the sea on stone is the sound of breaking glass,
that long stoop, glass-green,
holding the light in its pitch, then crazed, then gone.

*

They move slowly because the air is scant
and the ground unsure and the skyline a drawstring.
There are fires under the cloudwrack.

Shut

Days locked off. Windows blind side out. The world
unapproachable. There's a palette for this:
red shading to blue, where blue is a shawl of ice . . .

*

They sleep the half-sleep of animals and wake
to shared silence. Night-fears hold up
in that cold light: clatter of blades, rook in a stone tree.

*

. . . and red the burn. They find each other and hold on
like walkers in a wood at nightfall who smell smoke and hear
the fire's cross-currents working the canopy.

A list

Haggard angels, the killer-stare of the clown,
how you might suffocate
in a moth-swarm, how something already empty empties out.

*

They are housebound. She makes a sketch where the room
sits in another room like a seed in a seed-pod.
The walls are grainy with fracture, the door unopened.

*

Bloodlines: they go back as far as they can
but there's never another life
where they might have met and come to a room like this.

Skyscape

They go in step. The day comes up behind them
like a stalker, what they said
returned as echo, what they did given in dumbshow.

*

The people I love, she said, that I love most,
seem always close to tears. What is it –
the fastness of the night? Is it where we live? I think it is.

*

Look up: contrails and weather fronts, cliff edges, meadows,
a coppice, streets, houses – for all they know – where people
hold each to each in torment or the expectation of joy.

Cradle

Evening sun in the hallway. They turn back.
It's too deep to step into.
Low voices, an oboe, dog bark. All the little secrets.

*

They settle down to drink, to sift through the albums.
Everything looks makeshift: sepia sinkholes,
empty skies, people lining up to be recognised.

*

And this is how it is with whisky: you see a bruise start up
on his ribcage or under one eye.
Her arms make a cradle. He falls through fathoms of light.

Lamplight

Now at her mirror, she looks beyond herself to find him
as he strips to the skin. This is to know him better.
The lamp has a blue shade: a chance buy, midnight blue.

*

She moves away. Her mirror image moves
almost in unison. Traces of breath on the glass, unwatched.
Her shadow by the door where he came in.

*

She puts her mouth on his. She feels his hands
as if they made shapes in water.
He wakes at night and the room is drenched in blue.

Fall

Dustbowls of the mind. Flashbacks to days of waste.
He shuts his eyes on a house laid bare.
A white bed in a white room.

*

That they are coded: certain words, paintings, music;
that a bird riding the wind
takes sun on the underside of its wings as they watch.

*

Last light reads as lost light, I saw as eyesore, blind eye / blind I.
The dream where they go hobbled
is a dream of falling, a stairwell opens to an open sky.

The book

Here is the empty house. They stand outside,
one at the window, one with a hand on the door.
Shadows run on the walls, and there are voices.

*

She tells him how it is when someone dies. Not someone
she loved, but she found the turbulence
in vacancy, stillness as gesture, the way silence takes hold.

*

Now she is 'in the depth of his embrace': this from a book
where someone 'must cut and run' and love's a pestilence
that 'winnows to the bone its chosen few'.

Sightlines

They share this – a riptide of fire over grassland.
He finds it first and tells her where to look.
What they choose to see. What it seems most like to them.

*

How a cityscape blurs in half-light, how a landscape blurs.
Skyline, treeline, tower blocks, rooftops.
There is nowhere to get to, or nowhere they want to be.

*

To stand by the sea. To feel its draw and drag. To speak again
of lovers who walked out against the tide,
are walking even now, hair gone to weed, eyes to sea-glass.

An exchange

Hers to him, a witch's ladder; his to her, a crucifix
once his mother's, her mother's and hers, a tiny Christ
rubbed faceless, rubbed to a wand, the shape of pain.

*

She turns her head to speak but doesn't speak.
He reaches out to touch but doesn't touch. A numb
silence lies between them. Look, their eyes are shut.

*

He feeds from her plate. She eats from his hand.
Bread, oil, cheese, wine. One glass
between them. Sacrament of lintel and latch.

In time

He is ghosting his second self, a rags-and-rattle quacksalver.
Now he conjures her up in baubles and ball gown.
Sashay and slide, tilt and tip, they dance the trickster-tango.

*

Their tokens are feather and stone. A pebble split by the sea
shows a demon-face, dark-eyed and warped to a sneer.
It sits in the cup of her hand. She neither moves nor speaks.

*

She holds his head and whispers: *hiss-hiss-hiss*. Their patois
has slant-words for subterfuge and risk, that might
be given in song or in mime, might frame the perfect lie.

Where they stand now

Tree as dead letterbox, rook as picket or spy.
They'll be found here from time to time. The weight
of sadness in their kiss brings on bad weather.

*

A gate onto a door onto a room where anyone
might sit at a window: music no consolation,
reflections muddled by twilight and firelight.

*

As if they found sightlines in sleep, as if
they sleepwalked to a deep drop, sleep
drawing them on, as if they might take that step.

Night. Night not attained.

[. . .]

. . . the night of our voices. Bitterness. A taste of copper and death. To embrace the grave and the unique, the inexhaustible and the word.

[. . .]

'My eyes. My eyes.'

Jean Daive, *Under the Dome: Walks with Paul Celan*
Trans. Rosmarie Waldrop

HALLWAYS & ROOMS

Room three

The room is empty. 'Seamless' might come to mind. He is suddenly tearful. Because the floor slopes away. Because the air is painfully thin. Because the walls are rhomboids. Because he can hear voices that come in from the street. Because he is alone in the room. Because when he opens his eyes he's still here. Because he holds a memory of this that won't come clear.

There's a door, but it can't be seen. He sits against the wall, chin on knees, arms wrapped round. If he were dreaming, it would be like this. He counts to a hundred, then counts back. He would like to talk to himself, but feels the risk. The door goes from floor to ceiling: imagine the weight; it will open to the touch, silent, and swing back, silently. The temperature in the room is perfectly even. He can whisper his name, that much is given.

*

This hallway is lit by a caged moon-lamp and goes to darkness.

Room seven

The women sit in a circle, between them a half-done quilt. They are sewing patches. He is here in the room but they pay him no mind. They talk in low, soft voices that weave and fold. He wants them to know him but can't draw their attention. He whispers his name but it's lost in the weave. (From somewhere, the sound of a pot-lid chattering.) The patches and scraps come at random, pick your pick. Their hands rise and fall in sequence, silent music.

Pattern of a labyrinth, meanders and dead ends, as if it mapped the hallways and rooms, as if this room were part of it. He steps those steps: they bring his face to the wall. (From somewhere, a radio tuned to song.) He notices, now, that the room is windowless. One pricks her finger and licks the blood away. A web of voices: he is dumb. He listens for his name; it doesn't come.

*

This hallway is lit by a caged moon-lamp and goes to darkness.

Room nine

Graffiti in several languages. Indelible. It might be chanted or sung: he imagines voices, but women and children only, singing doubt, singing despair. He stands at the centre and turns with eyes half-closed so the words first merge, then pull apart. Some are broad, bold strokes in black, some have ragged runaways from the daub. Signage as rhythm, signage as pulse, as gesture, as loss, as breakdown. As forcefield. The ink is wet, the paint is fresh.

Notice the footprints. Notice how they go concentrically to the middle. Notice the ceiling, unmarked. A window sketched in, latches and bars, view of a black moon on the rise. No days and dates crossed off. No pleas or prayers as you might expect, might hope for, perhaps. The room carries an echo, unsounded, cacophonous. Now look. Look. Smudges something like hand-prints. If he stayed long enough in the room he would understand.

*

This hallway is lit by a caged moon-lamp and goes to darkness.

Room thirteen

Man, woman and child. They are cast as the wretched of the earth. They have that bombsite look, near-bloodless. The man is mid-forties, the woman mid-thirties, the child is ten, skinny, straw-blonde hair, eyes colourless. They haven't taken their clothes off in weeks. They are speechless. They turn towards the wall, raising their hands. They make shapes in air and their shadows close in on them. The wall is brick: a rough cement overlay against their fingertips.

There is nothing to be said or done. You would think they're related. They're not. They break position, fold in on themselves and go to ground, heads together, backs turned to some remembered wind. It's cold in here and, as their shadows fade, grows colder. He can feel the onset of night in the corners of the room. The woman bares her teeth. The man mimes smoking a cigarette. The child's repeated gesture is also hand to mouth.

*

This hallway is lit by a caged moon-lamp and goes to darkness.

Room seventeen

They are moving in slow circles. They are dressed for the occasion. They hold cocktails and, when they're not talking, sip. They almost fill the room, more or less evenly-balanced: women to men. A flunkey gives him a frosted glass and squirts a haze of vermouth onto the gin. (From somewhere, popular classics played near-inaudibly, tune-soup.) He isn't spoken to, though a red-haired woman smiles. She is mannequin-perfect, hips and lips and tits and nails.

Their voices run under the music. It is like a round dance though they never touch. Why do they resemble one another? When will the shapes they make – near touch, side step, glide by – cause them to slip? How do they speak without speaking, look without looking, move to stay still? The red-haired woman turns towards him and tips her drink an inch and, for that moment, holds the stage. What would it take, he wonders, to release the room to rage?

*

This hallway is lit by a caged moon-lamp and goes to darkness.

Room nineteen

... what you want and what you need will not be clear to me until you've gone and might never be clear to you. Some of what you know I also know some of what I know will be lost on you. The voice precedes the man who is tall, is bearded, is loosely dressed, has wind-shocked hair, is criss-crossing the room at pace, who lets his arms hang down, trains his gaze always to wall or floor. *You know of that which was and that which is but not . . .*

. . . that which will be although if you hulk a hare and shed the guts or be mirrored in obsidian or rake the embers of a fire set for the purpose then something of fear perhaps some depth of darkness some trace of a deathshead grin standing in for the lover you hoped to conjure up. He stops, face to a wall, and shuts his eyes. A shudder grows and beds at the nape of his neck. . . . *mirrored in obsidian . . . there . . . there . . . standing in for the lover you hoped to conjure up . . .*

*

This hallway is lit by a caged moon-lamp and goes to darkness.

Room twenty-seven

A bird, or shards of light. A bird. Its wings clatter the walls. It lifts to corners, then veers away. It skims the roof, goes side to side. Nowhere to roost. Nowhere to land, as if the floor were birdlime. No sight of the sky which is, he thinks, the root of its madness. It's said that milk will sour. It's said someone will die. It's said there's no defence. He sits down. The bird flies over him, then comes back to his shoulder. All that frantic movement draws to stillness.

A memory, half-held, of a dream in which he is lost in a country unknown to him, people unknown, language unknown, first a cliff-road above the sea then, in the way of dreams, a city, broad avenues, high-rise steel-and-glass, traffic moving evenly and soundless. The dream remade, his being lost its purpose, the way back gone. The stillness brought this on.

*

This hallway is lit by a caged moon-lamp and goes to darkness.

Room twenty-nine

[Writing on a white wall. Black on white. The white is silence; it corrupts the black.] *All roads abandoned. I looked out from an upper room. Clear skies and limitless silence. I went from room to room closing the doors. The keys had gone from the locks.* [There are words that must be guessed at, others stand out.] *Food, water, books, some of what was in my secret place: old birthday cards, dice in a wooden cup, the blue morpho in its small glass-fronted case.*

When the sun dipped behind the cathedral spire, I was miles away. [The lacunae trace a pattern that might be mapped.] *The evening before I had sung 'My Love in Hiding'. They agreed it was heartfelt. The windows were open and there came applause up from the street.* [Neat small capitals.] *I threw the dice to tell which way to go. I walked eight days, then saw a different spire and made for that.* [The white is silence; it surrounds the black.]

*

This hallway is lit by a caged moon-lamp and goes to darkness.

Room thirty-three

In here, a woman presents what might be a play without words, might be herself as installation. A nude, part nude: lighting draws a line a little below the waist, a little above the knee. She turns away and pauses, then turns back. Her only prop is what looks like plasma in a bowl of blood. Now a slow dance given in silence where her hands draw down sometimes to take the light. With her face in darkness, her hands must do the work. She falls to the floor.

A screen comes up. She watches the playback, watches from shadow in which her darker profile can be read: full-breasted, well-fleshed. The screen sheds bars of light; she turns, turns in the dance. She pours from the bowl; the caul slips from belly to thigh. Screen to black, then title: LA FIN DU MONDE. She speaks under her breath, as if to a friend, and laughs. No one's there. It starts again as if by chance. She goes to the screen, flicker-lit, to join the dance.

*

This hallway is lit by a caged moon-lamp and goes to darkness.

Room thirty-seven

A man beating a man. Take as read the cries of the man on the floor. Take as read the billy or bludgeon, the knout or sjambok (what you will). Take as read the indifference to pain as to reason. Is there, perhaps, a podium set to one side, a functionary, her lecture, 'The Art of the Beating'? She points out how blows are sculpted in air, mentions the stoop of the raptor, how the slightest wind will shift the topmost branches, the lift and stall of the prima ballerina.

Think on her further lecture, 'The Beating to Death', her key words 'mete' and 'tally' and 'assess'. Take as read the slow diminution of cries, the percussive crescendo, image of a conductor's baton: *poco poco accelerando*. Might she sometimes glance across, wanting to match her words to the action? When it ends, she lifts her head and laughs. Imagine her – hair tied back, eyeshadow, that touch of blusher, just as in all the family photographs.

*

This hallway is lit by a caged moon-lamp and goes to darkness.

Room thirty-nine

An odour thick as smoke. A room at the top of a house in a backstreet in a city in a country not his own. The memory is awkward, rough-edged: whose house what city where? He remembers magazines and trinkets, remembers a Roman blind, a book open and face-down, pages torn out. (From somewhere, what sounds like nothing so much as a shunting yard.) An easy chair, a footstool, maybe a bed. He is wearing that old coat and a ring he lost then found.

As if a misfit; as if at one remove. A nickname used as an alias. Winter light, it seems; a chill; the image of a window cast slantwise to the floor. He was pacing the room, this room, and now he stops, head to one side, eyes closed, hoping to hear someone speak, then put a face to the voice as a way of finding himself. He knows that smell but not what it is. He has misremembered the book and the Roman blind: they come from another time.

*

This hallway is lit by a caged moon-lamp and goes to darkness.

Penultimate room

A table at the centre. On the table, a porcelain hand, index finger raised slightly at the knuckle. A hand on a table, the arrangement under a pin-spot. Light taps the lifted knuckle. He moves in, then stops. Something, but what? – because he yawns, as a dog would, or an ape, in fear. Plain unmarked wood, white porcelain. Table at the centre of the room, hand at the centre of the table. Nothing more to be said. He shuffles back a step and shakes his head.

And looks up. The one painting in the room is small and plain, plain blue, a clear blue summer sky painted *en plein air*, no cloud, no bird, no leaf, and done on a held breath. It hangs at eye level, lit from above. There must have been such a day, there must have been such a sky. The room is still and silent; the air seems heavy, it folds on him and sticks: a second skin. It is now that he starts to shake, and crosses his arms on his chest to hold the tremor in.

*

This hallway is lit by a caged moon-lamp and goes to darkness.

Room one

In the far corner, a grille. Were he to go full length and peer down, he would find dark water, deep. Were he to stand over it, he would feel its draw. Were he to listen, he might catch something of the faint, persistent music that plays between here and there. Were he to speak into it, his voice would be transformed. Were he to fall asleep beside it, he would come to a starting point he is unaware of ever having occupied or left.

The room is windowless, but there comes to memory something like nightfall, something like dawn. Night birds are silent, the birds of daybreak call, that much comes back to him. Sunrise is a handspread of light, sundown an extravagance. How long? He tips towards weeping but holds back, fearing the sound. How long? An itch runs under his skin to eyeballs and fingertips. He holds his face to the wall.   How long?   How long?   How long?

As if there were shadows. As if some other shadow might fall on his. As if a shadow-hand might touch his own. The hallway was lit by a caged moon-lamp and went to darkness, that comes back to him. It starts to rain, or seems to: deception is some of what's left. He walks close to the walls, touching, as he goes, the graze on his face, listening to his footfalls, the rhythm of his breathing as in sleep . . . and here's the grille, dark water deep.

*

[. . .]

You can fasten your windows and doors against nightmares

but at dead of night you can hear them

as they pass through the wall.

The German Legends of the Brothers Grimm

AT THE WINDOW

A man at a window. A man neither young nor old, but he feels the press of death. Most often there at first and last light or in the deep of the night woken by dreams. Because there is no one to hear him, he sometimes speaks out loud, a fractured monologue, sometimes a word, sometimes half a line. Much of his life has been spent at windows. There was a time when he was known for it. Now he is not so closely known. What he sees is both familiar and strange. It has come to him that 'seeing is believing'. It is an attic window and gives a long view.

How this pale dawn light floods in from the skyline.
How it seems almost at times to fail as if it might
fall back to midnight's deep blue-black: as if it should.
I am given over to dreams that say what's mine is mine.

I dreamt I was at this window and here I am
not dreaming, or so I think, though something stays.
Dream has its flow, pain its own song to sing.

Rain sets a long graze on the glass. I know
nothing can come of this and this will pass.

Creatures of the peaceable kingdom
huddle on the lawn. When they lean on one another,
their colours bleed. Their hides are priceless. Herds
are a cash crop, stript and saleable. All this

called by the garden goddess: she alone
stepped in among them, naked and dabbed with grime.
Birds fly low and settle the silver birch.

This will resolve in time, the vision harden
to a bas-relief that fractures at the touch.

My father is walking the boundary, lost and found
in death much as in life. He takes his time
on unfamiliar ground. He has his faithful wife
to hand: army-issue Lee Enfield 4 MK II, his wound

half-healed and open to the air. He'd like
to down the roosting birds in turn and hold
their corpses as they cool. What to repair his soul?

From first to last, cruelly used and cruel.
What to restore all that was filched from him and lost?

The garden goddess has a heavenly heavy arse.
And a cutting eye. And spit like syrup. Her gift
is miracle or burden or curse. All three.
It was love at first sight as anyone might guess.

Fragments of flint she stores. Fragments of bone.
Insects swarm to her. The tell-tale dint
of her footprint in London clay is there and gone.

Each day I look for her; each day, at first, I fail.
She stares up at the window, all but lost in green.

Sea-ice or lightplay? It gets to the door – or will, soon enough.
Roar of a bull-seal stranded, cry of a red knot stranded.
Whatever was rare is dead. All else is set to fail.
Whistles and drums, armies of Armageddon nose to tail,

each acronym a blood-pact, each flag a shroud.
Hucksters work the slums, bring in death's entr'acte
where the poor die drunk and laughing, where flesh for hire

goes broken to its bed, where children spew the air . . .
Lightplay as token. The skyline shrinks. The weather worsens.

The wrong choices return to remind me. Their morning song
carries the flat, rack-toothed whine of a bone saw. They line up
along the borders (aconite, hemlock, Jack-in-the-pulpit)
expecting to find me here at the window, whisky-sick

and ready to own up. The soil is sown with ash and grit;
there's fellowship in that and mourning, undertone
of grief, a subtle ache, soft madness like a blush,

things out of reach and out of sight and done,
a door swinging shut on an empty stair that night.

It comes at the dead hour; its fingers go to my mouth.
It comes at the dead hour; its fingers go to my eyes.
In the pit of night and its hand goes to my heart.
It is cold. It is glass. It is still. Its held look hardens.

Music up from the garden, broken cadence.
Music out of season, lost to itself.
Music soft and sudden, no reason, no defence.

When the sky clears there will surely come a small
flourish of rain, soft and cold and almost musical.

Here at my window a brace of crows, blinded
and hung from a gibbet. The brown hare is shot
as she weeps milk from her dugs. A hawk
is nailed to a fencepost. Shallow sleep at daybreak.

The wind is up. Saplings knock limbs and shiver. Shreds
of pelt and feather. Dreams, half-dreams,
a road out of here which only dreams deliver.

Ghost crow, ghost hare, ghost hawk, my face
dim in the glass, the window's sometime guest.

The dance of the garden goddess: against the grain.
Her migraine's a white spider, sudden when she bleeds.
She must suffer for allowing pain. Could close
your eyes, your ears, your mouth. No, I mean mine.

The music for this lies shallow, a touch will bring it on
and does. I think she's in tears. I think her dance
will make for a change in the weather, a month of rain,

herself hip-deep, the garden an inland sea. Her skin
carries a web of scratches from the firethorn.

Waking at three still drunk and still drunk now, influx
of bile, that inner stain, the prank dream plays on memory,
the broken smile that no fresh drink can fix . . . The sinner
dry-eyed, head in hands, another blank page to the file.

Shadow-theatre on the glass: the well-beloved one by one
then gone and all without a backward look: the farce
of love and forgetting, whatever luck called up and broke.

Whisky to gladden, whisky to beat the band. The face about face
of Christ Pantocrator, his drink in the other hand.

They are dreamstock, love's woeful recalls. A cold moon
leaves them white as birchbark. Their footfalls
are hidden histories. They bring their worst mistakes
with them, packed and labelled, all they own.

Memory quickens the heart, little treasons
fouling the blood even now, lies set in stone, a locked
door beyond a locked door, spur of the moment desertions.

Moonlight builds a stage. Each scene is bloodspill and scar.
What am I wanted for? Moonlight builds a cage.

The river from here is next to nothing much.
Up close it's monstrous. Already victim-rich,
it wants to haul you in: eyes in a caul of net
and water-weed, death-knot, a rack of bones

that shifts with the tide and forms, re-forms,
in broken simulacra. Those visions
never repair, never relent, no, they resort to dreams –

underwater drumming, bone on bone,
river at the full, blind eyes that find you out.

He comes as dusk is deepening, or else
in the bottomless hollow just before first light.
If I'm sleeping, he somehow wakes me. I think
he might have things to confess, tiptoes across

a patch of slash-and-burn where something grew
that was said to poison the air. He can touch but not hold:
sure sign of a life gone to waste, a life half-lived.

He is unloved, even now, even in memory, and the worst
yet to come. Daylight now. He is wan and shadowless.

Dancers go hand over hand on the riverbank path:
a saraband, which I take for a danse macabre
where death comes slow and stately. They are masked
though their smiles still show. Don't ask why. Don't ask

how music goes between them, unsung mystery, or when
they will falter and stall and part on a backward look.
First silence, then tidewash, then birdcall. It strikes the heart.

If they unmask, I might know them, might fall asleep
then wake another day to find myself part of the dance.

My thoughts are so fierce I sometimes mistake them for dreams.
'Where will I find you,' she asks, 'once you've gone?'
Nothing is what it seems. Each line a phantom limb,
my image locked off in the glass, my stare a stain.

This lyric flourish, this tricky deal with pain, this do or dare
has been my life, so find me pitching knucklebones
that clatter back from the wall where the weakest must go

me, not least, wheeled out white-blind, clutching my last
book – *Confessio* – blame and blight now signed and sealed.

Sin eater, stalker, someone I used to know whose sorry look
skewers me now, hophead, wife-beater, fast talker, barfly,
sixth son of a seventh son, in your best black, in your high hat,
refugee from the funhouse, gravehound, crook, outcast,

I can see that you don't throw a shadow, I can see
that your bony self barely holds up, the sad stoop
of your shoulder, how your face folds and falls to tears.

You were never what you seemed, never more
than shyster, trickster, unschooled in the language of dream.

I know I am waiting for dawn (whisky all but gone)
to have sight of the iron bridge, to find myself
halfway over, to feel that drag in the yoke of my shoulders,
a thing gaffed up from the edge, some snag in a weir.

There is a weight in me of sadness that will not lift.
People close to me are touched by this and marked.
Q: Is it all that will be left of me? A: As now, it's all there is.

Suddenness of love is heartshock or gift or both.
As now . . . (As now.) Cloud-shift. First light. Last drink.

A funnel of darkness goes to the vanishing point
where the city glow shuts down: infinite liminal.
A low note, slow, holding beside the limitless waste
of light, takes a lifetime to travel back and set

a shudder in the glass where a man might sit
with a visitation of sin, sin's dark addition,
last line written, last penance made in haste.

And music comes to mind, again, again, that raid
on the furtive soul. A lifetime, it's said.

Angels swim in air above the rooftops. Almost dawn.
Almost-dawn-light. Blue half-light in the room. Perhaps
the voices of angels, these alone, are heard
only by the dying, that remorse is all they sing.

My face turns back to me; a flaw in the glass
will test what I think or write or want or love.
In this, a measure of grief, a measure of grace.

Beauty and dust are so close. Sin and delight.
If my heart stops now, stops now, I will hear them at last.

They discovered that in this house

there is a room with barred windows

to which no door exists.

Gustav Meyrink, *The Golem*
Trans. Isabel Cole

OF CERTAIN ANGELS

The Angel of Transformative Light

On her back, on the bed, arms raised, legs spread,
who did this, who dashed on a smudge
of lipstick, fanned her hair across the pillow, guessed

her wingspan, found a way to make a shadow's shadow
from the hard stark white of pinion feathers
against Egyptian cotton, who thought to allow that fusion

of lust and prayer, that fission, eyebright, fever-race,
then bring you in, a ponderous silhouette . . . *O!*
who gifted her the seven words now cut into your arm

ragged like a prison-house tattoo, who picked the lock
on this door of all doors, who set the cheval glass just so
to give her back to herself, up on all fours, that wide wingspread

mantling her smile and hiding her greed from God? Slow light
when she moves on you like that, smoke-light, water-light.
Leaving, she turns to share a soundless whisper,

a secret lost, white breath on empty air . . . *O!* in the full flush
of her nakedness, faint scent of fallen ash, walls scuffed
with light, her handprint at the cave-mouth.

The Angel of Lost Things

A Skara Brae of the mind, where she walks
from sun to shade . . . on either side, stone shelves
where what you thought lost is kept, each *item* bearing

the ache of estrangement, a ghost-limb, each
having forgotten the name it's known by and what it's for,
bric-a-brac set away from the island light

to keep it from spoil. This thumbstone will never
come back to you, but will be as it was in the moment
it fell from sight. If you sometimes reach for it

in memory, you'll bring a fingertip to her backbone.
All given over to chance: that loss on loss
is breakage in the pattern of your life: she keeps

a record, something much like a star chart,
tide table, notation of birdsong. If only you knew
what prayers and hallelujahs light the commonplace

and why she conjured up these low rooms, lintel and latch
under a scrim of turf and sand, to put the lost things in place
as if she had scavenged them from the tideline

and brought them safe home. There they wait,
suddenly mysterious, palmprints of claim and protection
pressed to the ceiling space. Goodwife-angel, she has them set by.

The Angel of the Surrogate Quotidian

As your lover throws back the sheet, unhurried
nakedness, walks to the window soft-footed, sees
a jay gather light to its wingspread, wingspread

of the angel (remember) who brought tokens, a sea-
washed pebble, holly, a handspan of driftwood, and sang
something known only to her that carried a depth

of mourning: grace to the new day's dead. In her satchel
bread, olives, wine. When she sets out that offering
her hands shape the air: a blessing; her wings

mantle the food as a hawk mantles its prey, opening
songbird or shrew, protocols of bloodspill, flesh
as sacrament (remember) bare bones to the wind.

As a man starts a fire in his garden. As rain shapes itself
to urban yards. As a cat goes between glance and glance
to arrive in the moment it leaves, beauty-in-stealth of Noh:

she offers herself to this as to the faint, half-expected
pain behind your eyes, to the ectopic beat, to the way
a stalled breath leaves you trapped in faultless silence.

Your lover turns from the window (remember) and lays
a hand to your face. She offers herself. Of course,
there is singing somewhere close. She is matched to the music.

The Angel of Delinquent Poetries

She has you by heart and gives you back to yourself
in those few moments when she comes to lie beside you,
when you touch her, when your touch puckers her skin,

when she half-turns to speak and her wings gather evening light
setting a shadow-clutter on the wall. (The wall is innocent
of all else.) She has found the damaged music in your lines

and sings it without fault, image and abstract
telling the pale processional of your life. Sometimes
she reframes it to sing of herself: womb envy, night vigils,

the debt she is owed by God, a better poem than yours;
it questions flesh and what flesh brings to love . . . then stops
on a broken note, a woman, suppose she were a woman, stifled.

This poetry is ruinous: her face a map of scars, her wings
crow-black, her fearsome waking dreams of Paradise: a legend
among her kind, its windows and mirrors, roads drawn

to a vanishing point, white skies, a driven silence . . .
She harvests cancelled lines, abandoned drafts, those words
that carry more weight of pain than the poem could hold,

fragments of a songline that brought you here
unknown, unknowing, abandoned to chance,
the timelock on your life coded to her palmprint.

The Angel of Death Knell Chorales

Bloodless, blue-lipped, head shaved, is how you see her.
She brings with her, from that other place,
the voices of children, harmony-in-heartbreak

bright notes ringing bare bones, in measure of pain
unmistakeable, a boy treble set against
a muffled bell, her sure hand fills and shapes it.

The descant is rainfall. They sing – she sings –
for Shelley drowned and burned at Viareggio,
Lamia in his pocket, Trelawney caught up his heart

from the brands; she sings – they sing – for Paul Celan,
in off the Pont Mirabeau and washed into a weir;
they sing – she sings – for Hart Crane, numb

to poetry (meaning as good as dead) spectacular
in flight among the birds mobbing the boat.
Will someone, you wonder, *ever catch up my heart?*

The Angel of Cureless Anhedonia

A painting in which she gathers a shawl of nettles to her throat;
a poem where she is made barren by longing; this duet
for alto and sax, marked *lachrimoso* – sadness

as rhythm and flow, as slippage of colour, a word
spoken in slow repeat, soon becoming meaningless,
an errant smile developing toneless laughter . . .

She enters by rain-light and draws you in. She has a black
book on you, notes of how accidental pleasure
left you staring back at yourself from a shopfront window,

of a letter to someone unnamed, asking to be told again
of coming ashore on that island known for its music
and sunsets, of leaf-shadow on clouded glass

that first morning, of flame kindling the tip of your cigarette
as you lift the perfect Martini. (In that same book
is a sketch of you on your knees in simple light.) She sleeps

at the foot of your bed and when you wake at the dead
hour, speaks to you as to a man on a ledge stranded,
as she is stranded, between heaven and earth, and set to fly.

The Angel of Risk and Regret

Airborne in a stairwell or taking a blind bend dead
drunk across the cats' eyes: her wild laughter
as she laid a hand on the wheel and brought you back,

same hand that held you steady as you stepped
out on the parapet, when to walk on air
with river lights cutting the darkness was to set

risk against anger – and the urge to nudge you over
a ghost-gesture in her: to let you hold your line
on a midnight road, or prompt a curse to a homicidal stare,

the impulse to sin of the harlot saint, some trace of lust
the desert sun could not burn off. That vision corrupts.
It takes her to the edge. She walks on air.

The Angel of Furtive Eschatologies

Hand in hand to the boneyard . . . that half-heard
seamless note – the city's tinnitus – gone
as if she'd flipped a switch, nothing between you

and the image she allows of the bloodless dead
clawing their coffin lids. The thought amuses her,
just as she smiles at headless stone angels

in the rising mist, at *'Tis death is dead not she*,
at the drum roll of thunder that celebrates your arrival.
She calls on the dead for a dance

which you somehow see, subtle music in bones
as they go between markers that bear their names,
until she sends them back. None of this is cruel:

as you remember the dead so the dead
remember you, things are what they are, she allows
sight of them whole and undisturbed, or their wounds

showing livid and wet, or a barcode of illness
die-stamped at the quick, or where
they gain themselves, remade, in the sight of God.

Now, in this dry storm, faux-apocalypse, you tremble
to join the dance. She will play for you on a bone aulos.
On the way back she will touch you, softly, to slow your heart.

The Angel of Stopless Sorrow

At this time of night, in this depth of darkness, the house
brings in the sound of someone weeping, weeping
and sometimes speaking, that low music fading

to a single note as you go from room to room
where the voice left traces, so you collect
syllables that rearrange to *end of days* or *flood and fire*.

Here is what would be her footprint, what would be
her image on glass, a shed feather, the shape
she would make in air, unmistakeable for its stoop, the line

from lowered head to breast to hip to knee
sorrow's golden mean. Now take her scent, nightstock,
tart like her yearly bleed; she draws you on

as if gesture could pattern the silence. In one account
she is dark-eyed and reckless, in another a dove tamed to the dovecote.
Her burden is inexpressible love. She has forgotten your name.

The Angel of the Skyborne Mirage

She catches you in the corner of her eye and reinvents you
as a refugee soul in need of some measure of love,
drawing you in and into the scope of her wings,

the close edge of passion, her body dark angles and deep
scents in which you might suffocate:
that feather-cradle, that aphrodisiac musk . . . The mirage

only sustains by your belief in her and hers in you:
sometimes cloudwrack, unfallen rain, patterns of light
refracting to a hall of mirrors that returns you to yourself

as victim or lover or starveling or vengeful child,
sometimes a web of streets abandoned
to patterns of light that blur to reachless distance,

sometimes a long perspective of rivers and bridges,
skies pearl and featureless, the water showing patterns
of light and the image of a man in torn reflections.

She works these changes, and more, in God's delay.
If you find ash on the heel of your shoe
you have come back (be sure) to where you most belong.

The Angel of Venereal Nocturnes

Stay close: when birdsong dies her song comes in
on a single breath, and you think water-flow, or how
still air is stirred by flight. Her voice is low

and holds a seamless note that trips your heart,
the burden sin-through-pleasure, the line-by-line much like
some black-book version of the marriage vow.

She stoops to bring you on, her gaze held hard
as a lover might set a dare, and the song, as it leaves her,
falls to flesh and the Devil, her secrets and yours caught up

in that slow music, your memory and hers of desire, of risk,
of betrayal both pure and simple. She will sing into remembrance
the girl with the rosary on her knees by firelight,

or the other, good with knives at the kitchen counter, or
the garden goddess looking up to your sun-glossed window,
blood-beads plucked on her skin by the churn of bramble.

Tokens, touchstones, a sacred heart on the sill, a fish, clean-scaled
and slit from nock to gill, blood-beads smudged
onto the palms of your hands. And now she has you on stall,

your suddenly empty eye, your indrawn breath, her song
a pendulum, illusions of aphrodisia, of morning-light
in the room where she first found you, alone and terrified.

The Angel of White Silences

In the world's turning there comes a moment of stall,
earth's apnoea, when the unborn and the new-dead
gather a silence; it is all she knows of Heaven.

Silence as the knife is taken up, as water
grows still, as hope turns back, as thought
shuts down, as a door closes never to be opened.

The perfect lie in its cage of silence, the dropped
heartbeat that marks the wedding-vow, the bird
as it catches rising air (*O!* she is at your shoulder:

half turn, her breasts graze your arm, you see how well
she carries her scar) an echo – your name – emptied
into itself, that nerveless silence which is the silence

of the mad, a dream narrative broken, a word
in the mouth of the unearthed skull, a man
in the soundless acres of his leap from the parapet.

'Find me out in that last moment' (your whispered prayer)
'You will never find me penitent, but find me out
in the deep white silence of my death where I come to nothing . . .'

At the still centre, her vision holds: of fire
on the sea, fire at the core, at the end of the ending day,
silence of a dying star as it folds to whiteness, she waits on this.

The Angel of the Good Death

She brings to a white room a white bed. Full moon
to the bare window. White silence to empty walls.
A white book, your last and best, lies where it fell.

She is wearing one of the lost things: a jet
choker retrieved from the rack of days
when the near-world dimmed and words

shed their meanings and memory turned on itself.
She waits in the room. Hers is the only scent, a thin
reek, which is desire, which is death-sweat,

her gift to you when the time is right.
That white light, a pin-spot, comes from her diadem:
if you were here it would find you centre stage,

a man self-abandoned, speechless, blind, holding
a vision of fire on the skim of the sea, holding a line
of music, uprooted, that plays back, and back again.

She will come with whisky when you call for it.
She will come to you naked in the small hours.
She will come to your funeral, as promised, *en deuil blanc*.

Jeder Engel ist schrecklich. Und dennoch, weh mir,

ansing ich euch, fast tödliche Vögel der Seele,

wissend um euch.

Rainer Maria Rilke, *Second Duino Elegy*

SKIN

Sub rosa

The upper floor of the whorehouse carries scents
that swamp the corridor. You go knee deep
in Nuit d'Amour and rut, a stench you'll hold
in memory and soon come back to as you try the door
to a room where your wife lies naked in a drench
of sorrow, whose life of want is now a life of prayer.

A player piano hammers nonstop ragtime. Burattino
waves you through. LE CHOIX DU JOUR is what you want
as always, as always more than you need: petite cocotte or hag,
but cut to fit when most are off the peg. She is solemn
as if love were in the mix. This night will feed your sleep,
white of her thigh, white of her eye, her sudden bleed.

Bonne bouche

You must eat it whole and hot; the tiny bones
will cut your mouth and blood richen the taste. You must
cover your head to hide your greed from God . . . and keep the best
to last because this will not come again. Then blot
your lips and save the stain. Sit back. Wait. As the heat
fades along your jaw, lift your plate and lick the drips.

Now lie awake tonguing the cuts. Now dwell
on how it was plucked, alive, feet snapped off, alive,
then drowned in Armagnac and brought to you
still smoking from the fire, sweet, half-raw, the sap
just tart enough to set your teeth on edge, the after-smell
charr and feathers and dung. Your lover is on her way.

Le'pra

White as snow, as snow as if – She goes from bed
to bath, unclean . . . unclean, your touch has left its mark,
your press, your sweat, your kiss, your cum, unseen,
unseen but sharp and strong, a patterning of hands
indelible as iodine, and even as she scours herself
your body still backs hers, your fingers on her face.

The dead leave tracks, she says. Invisible. But you can trace
a slight disruption in the air, also a taint. Impossible
to say quite what. Something of death's stew, something
of skin and soil, of slur and smear, foul breath. They lack
all kindness: their way of being dead. They lack all grace.
Your gain, she says, the dark deliverance that comes with grief.

Flense

First light. Do you recall your first sight of a hare and how
it sometimes goes by gobshite, wychesget? Did your first
love tell you that, who left a stitch in your lip, a thumbnail
sketch of herself on your glans, a trail of broken glass?
Do you see yourself hung by the heels, arms down like a diver?
Your eyes are blood-struck. You feel the drag of your hair.

Songs have been made for this slow death. They are voiced
by the blind. First cut, first cry: singer and scapegoat hold
the note and both at perfect pitch. But why,
when you think it through, is she nowhere to be found?
Lost in plain view, there's the catch; seen-unseen,
self-unself, gone into a hare and gone to ground.

Bare

Now she's at full stretch, eyes closed as when
she is listening to the sea and light flows on her,
blue half-light deepening; you catch the rest
of what she says though much is lost, as speech
on waking is lost, or speech in sleep, or voice in song
lost to the drawback of water hauling a pebble beach.

The place stripped down. Windows and doors. Table and chair.
A mirror that shows the skyline sometimes; sometimes
the room alone. Full stretch; she opens like a shell. Absence
is a weave, white/black. The close world breathes a smudge
as mist on glass. Silence deepens like weather and comes
to the brink. Something has left its shadow on the sea.

La Peau Sauvage

What you first see is the sheet tossed up and tossed
aside, which you take to be her shed skin, sole to scalp
and slightly soiled, which you have to test
for the small bar-code tattoo, for a fragrance of oil
in the tuck of her throat, but more for some trace of sin,
an act of betrayal retold as an act of grace.

Ghost-self, shadow's shadow, fold, refold, replace,
bed down on the last of her, the last you'll get
and least, go inch-by-inch, lip-to-lip, as she breaks
under you, blood-cast seamed with sorrow and regret
the imprint of her pulse, a line of light linking the seven
portals, this fragment you'll take away, fetish and token.

Jenny Haniver

Find her in dream, unnatural, feather and fin, eyes the colour
of sea, colour of sky, her gift to you your own name
spoken as if you could own it, tide-drift, wind-drift
bringing you to a soundless, sightless vacancy, freefall,
deep-dive, air and water forcing one another as you strike
the edge of night, blind and deaf and lost but still alive.

Stepping out of the shower, water to air, pearled, soft-
eyed, she is numbed by memory: how her fear
of falling is also a fear of drowning. Your face by hers
in the mirror, too near, too soon – she hasn't yet
found the full depth of her fall which might
never come if you lay hands on her like that.

Freggio

Silence shelves in the room, hard-edged. Dawn comes
as a palimpsest, stark-white, faces drawn and deleted.
She sleeps; you watch. What do you think of her –
that she's held in night-long dispute with the Bitch Goddess,
that she breathes in time with wave-break,
that she'll wake to an unexplained version of herself?

She breathes in time with the sea and wakes to downpour rain
shaping the window. No gain in that. Her dreams
lie skin-deep; you'll find them with a fingertip. The Goddess
came and went leaving on her a wound she now protects
with a close-cupped hand. That ragged sound is birdsong,
some tell in the rise and fall you'll never understand.

Scena

Her dream-book opens on a cry. So much lost, all else
corrupt or broken-backed. Threadbare narratives, thumbnail
sketches of Pulchinello (mad), Venus in Furs (wide-eyed), a fool
lopsided, set on a shaky underscore: cliff edge or tideline.
Sleep is a bridge that might, might not, hold up.
Out here at the midpoint, stalled, you are unrecoverable.

Something somehow building in the corner of my eye a shape
blurred by burning a junkshop where I search for what
was mine going by touch a wood become a sea become
a field of rape (this next page torn out) *some creature*
slinking through backstreets a man walks with me his bones
clank (this page and this page too) *I go naked in crowds.*

Rapture

It will be fire, it will be fire, it will be fire . . .

Walking through fire, firewalking, fire as pathway, as doorway,
as eye-of-the-needle, when daybreak is firestorm and sun-
set wildfire, whole cities hauled by fire, woodland, hillsides, this vision
of yourself as fire's good companion, custodian of the firepit, keeper
of the flame, of balefire, teller of tales where fire consumes its core,
where creatures of fire remake and there's movement in the sea.

Heretics staked out in the sun to scorch: here in your chapbook;
a prophet set on a pillar blinded by light: accounts of this;
priest and victim stilled and waiting on sunrise; the devout
white-eyed from bareheaded worship. In Greek high summer,
thin-skinned exquisites oil and turn and tan. Later they lie close,
folding into their heat as they fold into their flesh.

Via Lucis

Grünewald: Unterlinden Museum

It is to put the torn body of God-made-man in open view,
webbed and spoiled, it is to offer him as trophy, to start a lurch
of lust in all who stand as if at the foot of the cross, it is
to witness their laughter, their slow dance hand in hand,
which gives them sight of the hanged man's ragged back,
gives sight of his shuttered face against a gathering sky.

Your lover is on her way. She has packed for a journey.
Your lives deflect and collide like broken paths in a wood
where you make a slow dance hand in hand as you must
and loss the ghost of the dance. This is the cost: to touch
and turn away, to be featureless, to go by another name.
It is why you wait for her in a place of love and pain.

Vermin

Fox invisible in a cloudburst, rat collecting itself in in the broad
light of day, crow in fast from deep sky; there's no filth
they will not go to it's said, so think the worst: uprush
of blood in the henhouse, black bag of disease at your door,
a lamb dropped in snow and crow is there for the eyes.
Their footprints go before them, their bloodlust kinks the air.

Gallows branch, bow-trap, pole trap, foxpelt nailed
to a toolshed door. More fool you to think of it
now here at the shoreline as she tells you again how things
were and will be, the lie you depend on, turn three times
and spit and wish. The sky drawn down to the sea
makes a mud-cloud. Shoals of tiny white-eyed fish.

Nigredo

What goes to decay as if smoke had spread under the skin
darkening to charcoal, a black scab that will not shed but lifts
bringing with it the flesh uncooked weeping serum and you
untouchable, unforgiven, your shadow at night still sharp,
debt of sin wherever you look, names and places, eyes
and mouths, a rolling blur, but soundless, soundless in sorrow.

Your shadow at night, stolen from lamplight, reckless.
It lifts you and sets you down in another place. And this:
the scars that pattern your body are all that's left
of a fire-language long since lost, loops and bars, a codex
closed to meaning except for SEA and FLAME and NAKED SKY.
A night among nights when you pray and surrender your name.

Man On Fire

Tim Shaw: collection of the artist

Nothing to see save for a backdrop much like dawn light
pale and perfectly-chosen; nothing to hear
save for a restlessness much like a gathering wind. Perhaps
you've just woken, perhaps you've woken to witness
what happens next: a sudden press, the man at full tilt,
but held in the moment, much like exemplar or token.

And a silence making ready for when the vision breaks
as bare bright tips of flame flake off into words
unreadable save for   *look   look   look*   the man burnt black
in the furnace of himself, soot gone to the bone, his bone-
white stare and voiceless pain, what you take from this and carry
with you, the plummy stench, the billow and drumbeat of fire.

Hairpin

The contortionist stands on her hands and does a straddle-split.
She looks at you and smiles. Now are you blessed (only now).
Triple fold, chest stand, hairpin, half-forgotten shape
of a harp, a harp that sings, will sing if you allow.
She dislocates: arms break unbroken: threads through
the subtle knot her legs have tied behind her back.

Your lover is on her way, held by a waking dream
of fire on the sea, but turns to thoughts of waste,
of widowhood, of a widow's mark cut like a spider-bite
on the lift of her breast. What harm if they were to meet
by chance, a trick of fate, backstage or on the tideline
and greet one another in joy, sisters under the skin?

Contagion

When, in that moment of turmoil, your own shadow fell on you.
When you made the night-drive home taking with you the rub of her scent.
When you found she had left her mark, a dapple-pattern of bruise.
When the itch in your blood ran like a sudden flush.
When you woke to a putrid scurf on your eyes and on your lips.
When you mirrored the fairground Fish-Man, gleam of blue-green scales.

A second skin. As close. As tight. It wouldn't shrug off.
Over moorland in snowfall and (somehow) the moon.
Damson and lemon yellow. A fading ache to each,
so that silk is a hair-shirt, so that plain air chafes.
Sightless. Speechless. Sunlight no help, nor poultice, nor balm.
Sideshow freak. Roll up. Roll up. Spotlit and named and caged.

Selkie

Her swimsuit dropped like sealskin at the tideline . . . She's naked
somewhere close by. Then she's halfway home with the fish.
There's music as planned, and wine. The knife is her knife. She starts
at the anal fin and goes to the gill. Goodwife. Sure hand.
You'll think she's marking the music when she nods to the beat of the sea.
This plays to memory. She is drinking to be drunk.

Imagine a slip of wind coming in off the skyline, so slight
there's almost nothing of it, and holding a shred of song
that only she can hear. The song is a song of death. Also of love.
Imagine a seam on her scalp where the fontanelle would be. She strips
to swim. Imagine, if you can, how she looks when she looks at the sea.
In that moment you are lost to her as she is lost to you.

Marsyas

Those who were there, not least the women, opened to his cries.
Two had been to the market. They peeled a peach and shared it.
Others brought bread and cheese and meat and whisky. A child
carried her birthday gift: a linnet, caged. From time to time she ran
a finger along the bars and whistled through her teeth. The bird
dropped its head. A man set up an easel some way off.

His tree took the wind, a shiver from crown to root, and when
the sky darkened, everyone looked up expecting rain
which was there and gone in no time – *drench* – and then the sun again
drawing all towards it. Some workmen turned up and paused to watch.
They understood: haulage, measurement, method. Next there came a lapse
as when water draws back; in that silence, then, the tree grew eyes.

Haute Couture

Now she is not herself and this green suppurates.
Not herself and this red is a weeping rash, this black a burn.
Turn back the sleeve. There is her occult tattoo, a card
from the major arcana *Zero: the Fool* and this polka dot
brings up a slow bleed stain-to-stain-to-stain.
Knee boots are calipers, lipstick a scold's bridle.

The mirror is set at an angle to take the sky; cloud-race, sun
snagged on the bevel, a ghost image stored in the glass:
unclothed and fresh from her bath. *Yes, here I am* . . .
The street's a catwalk. Sirens and lights and trash; a huddle
of city birds, feathers dredged in soot and silent, silent.
. . . *face to face, my sullen heart, my womb a grave.*

. . . skin must suffer before skin grieves.

Job 2:4, *Knox's Bible*

MIRRORS & DOORS

a soft collision

Look past your face to find her face, a shape in mist, but stronger now
as your face starts to fade, but first
a fugitive geometry where planes and angles merge; you feel

a tug: her image goes through yours, a soft
collision; she wears you like a shawl close to the mirror's brim, and then
steps clear, a new way of becoming lost.

You're left with ley lines in floor tiles, a door half open, the way
a curtain folds to shape the light. It takes
all you have to stand here, touchless, everything at your back.

The door throws a shadow, a shadow lies
on that, not darker, but the door's rhomboid is cut by that second shape
which is something like the spread

of a wing if the bird were hovering and held in the instant before
it dropped (which brings in the sharp
scent of moorland, running water, cleanness) and struck its prey.

as if there were birds

It is deep night, the curtain thrown back, the full moon held
dead still on the dark side of the mirror.
There are no words for what is happening in the silence.

It might be that you are sleeping.
Let's say you are, and in your sleep the dead go through
hand-in-hand, walking in time

to a half-remembered heartbeat; they bring a tremor to the air
as if there were birds in the house
flocking in a room beyond this room. Each of the dead will leave

a dab of breath on the mirror: dimness
of a passing thought, which might be that your back-to-back sorrows
will carry into midnights such as this.

in at the upper edge

In the hall of mirrors she is pregnant, wasp-waisted, gone
to a knife-edge profile, come
to stand beside herself, disfigured, a woman in pain or in love.

A line of light from the door
patterns the glass: kerbstones to draw her on and draw her down
but she steps sideways

to an eyeline warp and her face folds in a guern, shocked
to silence, the burden of words
too great to carry in this windowless house, her name

changing with each new self,
her shrivelled lipstick-smile drawn out from side to side
when a thing comes in at the upper edge,

gathering in fragments, and you see her reach for it
as she goes to the mirror
her disarticulation piece-by-piece glass-borne and glorious.

the soft knock water makes in pipes

Go to the half-open door. Open it.
Nothing. Half-close it. Something returns to the far side, shadow side:
scuttle-scuttle-flop. Silence.

It might be deaf-blind you think, survive on one held breath, live
on whatever is dropped and take
its liquid from the mist on mirrors. Little homunculus escapee.

It likes half-light and corners, it likes the butt-end
of hallways where sweepings get left, it likes the soft knock
water makes in pipes at night.

Is it there when you sleep? You don't know. Is it there now? You don't know.
There are rooms in the house
where darkness takes shape. It shares a dreamlife with the unborn.

a rope of pearls, a shift

Can you see the painting on the far wall
that the cheval glass reverses, how the reflection carries to the glass
in the door that opens onto the garden . . .?

There is an endlessness that excludes every living thing.
Time and place deferred: evidence
of the painting in which a woman sits before a looking-glass, her head

half-turned to the door, finding the windowpane
that takes her image. She is wearing next to nothing: a rope
of pearls, a shift, her hair lifted

from the nape of her neck. Because she is looking back the pearls
have caught the light, a razor-line
running from each to each. It is the same room and everything in place.

She has opened her shift
to the waist. Her skin and the pearls are a match. In all that glass
you are nowhere to be seen.

even now unspoken

The door stands open and rain is falling through sunlight. A day
of terrors. You take to your bed.
Creatures of rain and sunlight swarm at the threshold.

A sensation of falling although
you are lying still, a stone in the road. If the mirror could find you
it would show a man gone to ground,

locked off in himself. Dreams in daylight are dreams of self and shame,
your backstory told just as it was.
You watch from the wings that your dream-lexicon redefines

as the wings of birds that go to roost and sit
in judgment. Your blood stills. You lie in a drawn breath, a night-
closed flower, and the dream

is a freeze-frame: you and A. N. Other face to face, unseeing,
packed in silence, a word
between you even now unspoken. The sound of the rain

is distant drumming, a house
where you once lived, pen and paper laid out, a view of the garden
from behind locked doors.

sweet dark innocence

A flare in the glass is corpselight. You could find a face in that smudge
if you look. Don't look. The room
gathers round you and there comes a line of song: small detonation,

close to the heart, that you hold
in memory for the moment of its singing, sweet dark innocence,
and then forget. A word, barely spoken, clouds

the glass; you finger-write it; the word is 'widowhood'. A wind
gets up in the land of the dead
and brings a chill to the house. Were you to look (don't look) you might

see figures gathering at your back
but really they are nothing more than the way light falls and fails,
the way the silvering slips

and lets you through to a place you thought unreachable, horizons
drawn back to their vanishing point, skies
emptied out, everything parched and colourless and still. So now set foot.

held in the cortex

Here is the room, final room,
where he lies under white sheets, motionless, his head
centred on a white pillow, the door

left part open. He can hear what's said of him; he might be near
death, might have died, and those voices
held in the cortex as they tell one another his story

as he might have told it himself . . . See how
in this you allow yourself as 'him' and allow the scene and allow
those who stand in the angle of the door

watching moment by moment, some seeing him close, some
as if he has already left, indifferent
to rainfall, turning his back as the window takes his reflection.

Death is the dark backing

              a mirror needs

                              if we are to see anything.

                                 Saul Bellow, *Humboldt's Gift*

NINE

Note:

What follows is a reconstruction of certain passages from a notebook found among the writer's effects. Some pages had been damaged, removed, or scored out. Gaps in the text are not lacunae: they follow the note-form manner of the original. Nine is a magic number.

The first page torn out.

A page water-stained and blurred, as elsewhere; as elsewhere, some text readable.

– the riddle of how she came to me at the tideline   (of a sudden   in a drift of rain)   riddle: tall tale   from some other place: what place?   at her sudden arrival the lost things fell to hand

– Fool: the overseer in motley   nine colours to his coat   bringing his marotte to turn the tide   he is nine in fool-years (eighty-one) but limber chipper showing a full set of teeth in his grin   riddler   jester   perfect imbecile   his cackle and call   he watches the flight of birds to gauge the future: nine white gulls on a flawless sky

                                                            her thumb-stone witch's stone   rubbed smooth   (how she loves prophesy)   the birds throw a shadow on the surface of the sea   a pattern against the pattern of the waves they tilt and slide down the wind   sea on stone is a voice   the birds find a thermal   white silence   Fool has nothing to say

The next page water-stained. The ink has run.

– when she spoke of women at the foot of the cross   (a blood-bright line in the grain)   their measure of insignificance   that their love was graft   then my heart came loose

– a day of groundfrost   she went to the sea   *lustratio*   breast-high   stock-
still to the wavebreak   count nine   count nine again   washed by the run
of the tide   this then: to reap as rapture what love first sowed as pain

                                            emerged cold to the bone
pain is omen too: the way it flows   muscle memory of undertow   at the
dead hour it comes again   then she dreams herself back   the weight of the
sea on her   the birds lifting to a dawn-sky in multiples of nine   that one
moment holding in sleep   repeating   her body holding the pain   what
flesh can endure by way of love or want of love   her dream of cleanness
beat of the sea

                           her eyes gather the dark

– attachment to place is sourced through heartbeat   leaf-fall   a show of
moonlight on the sea where she stooped (without looking) to find her thumb-
stone

                              the road out opening in sunlight
rainclouds dipping down where sightlines meet   shapes that rise from sea-
fret   rooftops low to the horizon   music untraceable   all else is rootless
when she spoke of women at the treadle   at the wash   scarred   'tekken
bad in labour and the bairn come dead'   her face grew that same scar (burn-
scar)   it was a haunting: their voices for a moment   for a moment their
laughter   rare harsh music   their hands at the skillet pail grate cradle kettle
bobbin stove broom doorstep cradle

– the worst of winters   deep frost stilled the sea   she thought to sleep it
through   one hand folded under her head the other tucked up between
her legs   if I were to read her dream I might find Fool dancing to a sackbut

Fool as putto   Fool as maiden aunt   Fool playing ragtime piano in the
Chicken Dance Saloon

she rises from
her bath in a rich coddle of lavender
          sometimes she smells of fishguts and gin

A page defaced.

– the door stood open and the place was dark   cold wreckage of an aban-
doned meal   the abandoned phone   seawater tang and stain   the
abandoned letter   a scatter of knives and pans   a broken glass   nine
candles set on the hearthstone: winding-sheets right for scrying   the
abandoned book marked at the tale of Rawhead and Bloodybones   how
darkness thickens   how silence takes hold
                                        a night-wind rattling the
reed beds is music of loneliness   music of abandonment

– and her pen left out uncapped   the nib a scab of dried ink   one line in
the letter crossed through but readable: *if the mind were to go what would be
left of spirit?*   (which fell into the silence)
                              when she spoke of wise-women burned
or hanged or led in chains to the water   the witch's mark on them   her
voice grew soft   she looked away   as if shaping them in memory
                              I understood in that moment that
love's disguise is deep   unguessable

– onset of nightfall   wind in wires as I stood outside looking in   small
shock of late birdsong   cloudwrack somehow backlit against a sky
darkening to indigo   something beyond pause   held at pivot point
fermata   a single note under the pianist's hand   heard and stilled and heard
and stilled again   played first in memory   then in the moment   then
lost   as when breakage has somewhere begun and is already echo or guess-
work   as when starlight comes to us cold and dead   as when a simple lie is
enough to unpick everything

                                                            'weight of silence'
is what I meant to write: outside looking in

– when the falcon went to her fist it staggered her   the impact rode in her
and rose: there came a pulse to her womb at the sudden flex of talons on the
glove   the dome of the sky lost light and emptied out   the line of its stoop
on the air like a scar on glass   as she hooded the bird they came suddenly
eye to eye

– nothing to be given or given back   nothing owed or ransomed   but traces
of her everywhere   dates marked for occasions of sin   notes on the
harmonies of weather: the music of daybreak   on hierarchies of
angels   on the goddess (triple-formed) and torch songs   (Imagine – she
said – Persephone's *Cry Me a River*)   lights switched off to welcome days
of rain   grey fall sometimes struck through by sun and copied to walls and
floors   to let those textures in   to be under a weir   set on a riverbed
looking up at the slow shock of wavebreak   naiad   selkie   victim of the
ducking stool taking a first breath as daylight dims   the stool is brought up

empty   the mystery opens there   her tormentors come to wretchedness
the poem falls to the page

                                                    when she spoke
of those born in the caul she put (without thinking) both hands to her breasts

– a man hated his brother with a hatred so deep it lay beyond words   a dark
angel came to him: Whatever you ask I will grant   wealth   land   prop-
erty   health   long life   bliss   but whatever you have your brother will
have double   Said the man: Take one of my eyes
                    That's it – she said – the punchline – that's the payoff

Pages cancelled by means of marker pen.

 – a long cry sometimes at nightfall sometimes at dawn   not human
unless. . .

                                                    tacked to the
wall Dürer's *Melancholia*: keys   daemon   magic square   refutation of
mere sadness or commonplace despair   Summon your ghosts   (she said)
deal cards   turn the nine of spades and know it isn't what it seems   (is
sometimes what it seems)   candle-wax or cards or markings on a pebble
lifted from the sea   call the quarters   crystal and water then   or last resort
which is flame and a looking-glass

                                                    that cry
is neither vixen nor bird but something lost to itself   (this in a letter never
posted)   held at the pitch of misery   it lacks an echo   or it is only echo

– Fool has a heel-and-toe routine close-matched to the danse macabre   step
and step and step and turn and step   he wears an eyeless death-mask which
makes him look for all the world like you   (she said)   not a ring dance
no   a dance to the edge   and the cloudrace held   birdcall held and wave-
break held and rainfall   see people in the dance whose names are lost to you
women hurt by greed in the guise of love   men disfigured by hope   step and
step and turn but their eyes are still   step and step and turn he brings them
on   drum and whistle and drum he brings them on   the sea at their back
a lick of flame on the shore   mute chorus line   arms in a scissor-link   high
kick but their faces lock and their eyes are still   her vision   which might
be a poem opening out   not so much you   (she said)   as how I see you
                                        whistle and drum   the sea   a lick
of flame

– is she then a witch or was she ever? she has the heartbreak for it and the
weird: notions of gift in the way her touch is pain   is all but pain   as near
to pain as pain is to healing   she would watch the sea for hours: her thoughts
unravelling   bloodrush: stillness a turmoil   she has no sense of blame:
what she collects   what she brings back   falls to a pattern no one else can
see: detritus   discards   rejects   pressed in the pages of her notebook
a nine-pointed leaf known to bring sleep and subtle dreams

– a day of rain when I told her death

                the rain made shapes on the glass and her eyes soon closed

                        I told her death

        pearl light lining the room   soft   near-touchable when
she reached out

        I told her death

            the sound hooding us both
she lowered her head   her breathing slowed

        I told her death had been much on my mind

– the story of herself is simply told   childhood half hidden   solitary rage
unearthly dreamscapes   husband in the usual way   skillet stove doorstep
cradle

        she works with knives   the
shape her hand makes when she guts a fish describes a fish   when its eye
has whitened she takes it from the heat   parts skin from flesh   parts moist
flesh   lights candles   pours wine   breaks bread: goodwife   her secrets
are closely patterned to the ritual   a life in waiting beneath the life she lives
chosen unchosen   there are spells that aspire to prophesy   (under her
breath)   *dulce periculum*   she goes into hiding in plain view   her second
self close enough to touch
        rhythms of water break into her
small talk

– she goes out at nightfall when there comes unbidden the image of a hare
at full stretch over stubble day's end sunset through cloudwrack the last cut

[184]

someone crying the neck *jink-jink* there are men there to bring it down just as they will bring down hawks rooks stoats foxes spillage of fearful joy black bile they eat the pelt the tongue the snout feathers and talons paw and claw the pizzle viscera in handfuls blood clots swallowed whole marrow from the bones they eat the eyes like aspic like oysters dribbled off the shell teeth seamed with gore

nine in the killing field   nine   she has them in mind

– Fool canters along the shoreline   codpiece   cap-and-bells   he has questions to ask about straws in the wind   about corruption in high places about those who lie out at night and take the weather   about how money makes itself and comes to good   about the deaths of children   about codes of tyranny   also about tyrants   about nine and multiplicities of nine about how that translates as song   about pleasures of the flesh   about that place where the sun never quite comes up   about how the cogs of the world can slip and stick   about evil and contagion   about how pain fronts laughter   about the mechanics of loss   about what stands in darkness wanting to be found   about the exorbitance of sin   about cold blind fate about what is passed in a glance or might be missed   about the style and purpose of birds   about how the world has come suddenly to its knees about love and that pitch defileth   about the vagaries of light   about betrayal   about whose child he is whose fool whose jackanapes   to ask whether I had spent half my life waiting by water   and of her why she made that arrangement of stones and glass

– you put your mouth to my breast   (this as she opened the fish   her back
to me)   my nipple between your lips   I felt your tongue   at once it came
to mind: *caritas romana*   her gift   his famishment

Three pages spoiled.

– when she spoke of women defenceless against rope and brand   against
flame   against purge   women at barred windows   women lost to them-
selves   women whose wombs are ransomed: are given over   women
drawn to harm   women who gather to practise secret treasons   women
courting depravity   women who sit silent in silent rooms   who set fires
who allow breakage   who go each night to the same dream of horizons   she
quickened her step as if the road might take her to such a place

– when she spoke of it again the road was the one road back   softness of
coming dusk matched perfectly to sorrow
                              the sea touched-in
                                    much else invisible

– a fierce wind off the sea   the churchyard dead settle deeper into the blow
trees feel it in their taproots   sky bellied down to the line of the long horizon
wavebreak a hurl of collisions   shoreline huts shifting and breaking: tar-
paper and tin   the church holding the sound-surge   its echo as one vast
pulse flooding the nave   slamming back on itself   tall candles for midnight
mass   the *misterio* set up beside the altar

                              Christ as blood-debt   as magic
doll   sin-eater   invisible friend
                         He is the thick of the storm

– the female form   (a charcoal sketch)   is a pattern of flow   is rhythmic
(first from life later from memory)   the way self shadows self   the way
line develops harmonies   the way light returns shape to shape   (up on one
elbow   her back to you)   what you see   (seem to see)   is movement
you misunderstand it   what you hear   (seem to hear)   is the last word
spoken   you misremember it
                              naked she breaks from herself
the image is set behind glass: your gaze returned to you

– call and response   a capella   *Wha' hills wha' hills are those my love?*   a
log-stove stoked against the night   shapes held in the flame: Hob: beardy
old bastard   single malt   sea holly in a jar   candle   a fish laid out to be
opened   *natura morte*   the song disturbs the moment   if not it would fix
and we would never turn from it

– this is how it is now you are gone   (a black square heavily inked)   this is
my waking   (a black square with ties as if a blindfold)   this is how I best
remember you   (a black square)
     tapetum lucidum is how the night-bird kills in darkness   is how it cuts
a line of flight through woodland   is how it quarters grassland: because the
eye has mirrors

in this room of blackouts it settles on its prey

(her unsent letter
much said of wild desire and of the heart's corruption
much said of risk and of the heart's corruption)

as you settled on me then   sightless   soundless

– multiples of nine return to nine   nine as a constant   lynchpin of fool's
kabbalah   enneagram   nine circles   nine worlds of the Yggdrasil (she
made a list)   that stone breaks along the line of its grain is proof of divine
imperium   coincidence is proof: nature's counterpoint   a run of luck
(she made a list)

her movement from
room to room is a solo do-si-do   a shape that holds on the air   near-visible

– when the eggs were robbed the ospreys rebuilt at the southern end of the
lake   even so the nest lay bare

she went day after day   most often at dawn or
dusk   one time bareheaded as a storm came in

downpour   a
snag of lightning   the tree barren
grief-nest   grief-nest   grief-nest

– also tacked to the wall Klimt's *Woman with Cape and Hat*   where she
comes in from the dark and fades to darkness as you watch   alongside
Sickert's *Le Lit de Fer*   where her nakedness goes for nothing   (one meets
your eye   the other turns away   both mute)

              when she spoke of women in that way pressed she
mimed drawing a veil across her face

– a thousand steps to the sea   a thousand from there to the pub   a thousand
to the churchyard path   a thousand home   those footfalls find equivalence
in music   also in the erotics of estrangement
             glissando/orgasm

                    as a dove clatters
up the rise of a steep parabola   tips   glides down the other side
            as a woman in love is found out by the pitch of her voice

– a swerve on a wet road on a blind bend on a dark night   drunk or near-
drunk   stalled in a fierce silence   almost gone under from the shock of it
                  now in her mind's
eye: an old woman at the threshold   praefica   a song of mourning
                before dawn
she wakes to a ghost-vision of the thing that flew at the windscreen or stood
in the road white-eyed
      she takes herself to the long field   that silence is the gathered stealth
night-creatures bring to early morning dark
        she said   (it was years ago)   You have found me out   and
We are unworldly   and   Touch me there   and   Touch me there again

Pages torn out.

– there were rags of fog in low branches   (she wrote it down):   the sun
anchored to the skyline   I seemed to sleep as I walked and heard   as if I had
spoken it   a darksome house   (the rest came later   she wrote it down):
in that microdream I was walled up   grave-dolls trinkets voices of my
children strange music   disharmony of slow fracture   I woke without
breaking my stride   did I then   as it seemed   go face-to-face with myself?
                                                                I am given to spell-making
which some call prayer
                              (that last line scored out   but with a light hand)

– the *common* act of *fornication* now declares itself *musical* or *sculptural*   not
rare but *rarefied*   sometimes *a rapid of shadows*
                                                        She wrote: you are an ache that
goes to the bone   what am I to you?

– the perfect tension of liquid at the rim of a glass   her face in the meniscus
warp of witchery   nine in a night is half a bottle of gin if you go half-and-half
go lip-to-glass
                                        being that drunk can leave you sleeping
night-long head-down-arse-up   your despoiler long since gone   having
helped himself to your Parker Achromatic   the scent of *huile de lavande* still
clouding the pillow

– go-between   technician of the dead drop   sitting on the sea wall with his
two-scoop tutti-frutti   rag jacket   triquetra tattoo   Leichner teardrop
fool of the two-way track   stalled by passion's overload
                              in his mind's eye: a crow in a crow trap

– near-night   birds break cover in silence   her downlight on the page:
Holbein's *Dead Christ in the Tomb*   a stiff hauled out of the Rhine to play
the tortured Jew   N.B. slow creep of necrosis   N.B. eyes / mouth / finger
of the right hand   (she made notes) Kristeva on melancholy Dostoevsky's
shaken faith   pain still holds to flesh in this   shock not aftershock   foul air
not immanence   those at the foot of the cross   Immaculata: the Whore
(*who cannot wepe come lerne of me*)   what sorcery could change him (none)
what angel attend him (none)   what secret be carried from this place to the
next   high tide under a full moon   she went out to the foreshore   sickened
whisky to cut the bile
                        cadaver as meat rack   death as guesswork

– she knows something of the rat and what the rat favours   that it likes cities
for the waste and spoilage   that it lives only to eat and breed   that it brings
incurable illness   that when under stress it grinds its teeth   that it shapes its
world by emotional contagion   that a rat-king is fixed by sebum and shit   by
blood and piss
              she once saw a lurcherman break a rat's back with a mattock
                    packets of rice and lentils gnawed open   pawprints in flour
                        she set a glue-board baited with fruit of the season

A page given over to nine hare-scribbles.

A page cancelled in red.

A page left blank save for a clumsy thumbprint.

– a broken bone   a fall of ash   blindness such as nightfall sudden in a
shuttered room   deafness as the room were set apart and sealed to sound

                                        a bone breaking: how that felt
ash cast down: the way it reads
                            whether sight or sound or both: *felo de se*   that
darkroom flourish

– as when ice fields pull back   as when plague finds its way   (she made a
list)   as when drought poisons the soil   as when a swan bleeds from the
eyes   as when the sea lets go its hold   as when there come wild distortions
in nature
                                                then corruption
has gone to the quick   gamblers and wreckers arrive and take the light   the
air stitches a thin mist of toxins   the moon is caught at the full and locked off
what sounds like a blast furnace is weather in the offing   and fire-in-flood
and carnage   cities falling
                        as when every doorway gives onto a boneyard

                        as when a swan is seen to bleed from the eyes

[All pages after this cut from the gutter]

Acknowledgments

Salt Moon – photographs by Simon Harsent, poems by David Harsent – was first published by Guillemot Press.

A Clockwork Diorama, published by Fine Press Poetry, is a selection of poems taken from the sequence *Animals Silent in Darkness*.

Of Certain Angels was first published by Dare-Gale Press.

Nine was first published by Guillemot Press.

Other poems from this collection have appeared in *Agenda*, *Ambit*, *14* (Vanguard), *London Review of Books*, MMU's online feature 'Write where we are now', *One Hand Clapping*, *Salzburg Review*, *Six Seasons Review* (Dhaka), *Swedenborg Review* and *Times Literary Supplement*.

*

Page 67. 'Lost in the near' is a line taken from John Berger's description of Marthe de Meligny's sometimes marginal appearances in paintings by Pierre Bonnard. It is a phrase I have used elsewhere.

Page 144. 'Bonne bouche' borrows from David Leddy, who borrowed from Anthony Bourdain.

Page 171. I took 'corpselight' from Meredith's *Modern Love*, that strange, compulsive outpour of sadness and regret. The term, as used here, is a version of *ignis fatuus*.

A line on page 179 is taken from Edmond Holmes's sonnet sequence *The Triumph of Love* (1902).

A section on page 180 opens with a line adapted from Seamus Heaney. It's a line I have adapted elsewhere.